T0322070

# FITWAFFLE'S
# No-Bake
# Baking

**EASY OVEN-FREE RECIPES** *including*
**CHEESECAKES, TRAYBAKES** *and* **MORE**

## Eloise Head

EBURY
PRESS

# Contents

# ABOUT THIS BOOK

I can't believe I'm here writing a third book!

I just want to start by saying a massive thank you to everyone who has bought my previous books and continues to support me, as this wouldn't be possible without you.

The best thing about writing these books is seeing the photos of them in your kitchens, seeing what you've made from them and all the amazing messages I continue to receive. They always make my day, so thank you.

Now let's talk about this book, *No-Bake Baking*! I absolutely love this book. It's fuss-free, it's quick, it's easy and it's so much fun. That's really what Fitwaffle is all about. It's always been my mission to make baking non-intimidating and accessible for people of all ages and baking abilities.

I love a short ingredients list, even now I'm put off when I see a long list of fancy things I need to go to three different shops to get my hands on. This book has over 30 recipes that use 5 ingredients or less, and everything can be found at the supermarket. You'll find 50 recipes that are favourites from my social media, plus 50 that are brand new and exclusive to the book.

You'll find lots of different desserts and plenty of flavours from fruity to chocolatey and caramel-y to nutty, plus lots of popular flavours such as cookies and cream, chocolate hazelnut and speculoos.

If you follow me on social media, you will know how much I love a no-bake. I absolutely love making all different kinds of cheesecakes, and just chucking stuff in a bowl or pan, mixing it together, then sticking it in the fridge and letting it work its magic.

Plus, not turning on the oven can often save time and energy, and stop you and your kitchen from overheating in the summertime!

This book is packed with creamy desserts that are perfect for summer, such as showstopping cheesecakes, easy ice creams, trifles and milkshakes. It also has warm desserts that can be made in the microwave, such as chocolate brownies and mug cakes, plus lots of easy traymakes, stovetop recipes, small bites and truffles, such as rocky road, fudge, French toast, pancakes and even no-bake slices.

There's a seasonal chapter where you can let your creativity run wild, plus there's also a brand-new air fryer chapter, where I have included some fun, easy-to-make savoury recipes by popular request!

Now you may think I'm cheating by adding an air fryer chapter to a no-baking book (especially when you find out I've included oven directions for the recipes too), but I wanted to give you an idea of how to bake in the air fryer when you don't want to turn on the oven.

This book is partly inspired by my childhood years when my mum wouldn't let me turn the oven on unless it was totally necessary to conserve energy and also because she knew I would probably make a total mess. This would have been the perfect book for younger me, and I hope this books finds a perfect home with you too.

*Happy baking everybody!*
*Eloise x*

So lemony!

# ABOUT ME

Hi! I'm Eloise, best known online as Fitwaffle. I'm a recipe developer, content creator, bestselling author, all-round foodie and former fitness professional.

Let me start by telling you what Fitwaffle means.

I came up with the name about eight years ago when I was working full time as a personal trainer and gym manager. I was learning to enjoy all foods in moderation after a previously poor relationship with food. I'm a big believer in viewing health as an overall lifestyle, both physically and mentally, enjoying all foods in moderation and not demonising specific foods.

Fitwaffle encompasses my two passions, fitness and food.

The 'fit' part also means fitting all foods into your diet, and the 'waffle' part also refers to 'waffling on', because I tend to talk lot...

Food has always been a big part of my life. I used to bake with my great auntie when I was little. She taught me and my sister how to make jam tarts, fairy cakes, shortbread and so on. She also taught us how to make chicken, rice and peas, which I have to admit wasn't quite as fun as decorating biscuits.

It's my personal mission to help others learn to enjoy all foods in moderation and improve their relationship with food. It's also my goal to help people become more confident in the kitchen, by showing that baking and cooking doesn't have to be intimidating, making it easy and accessible for people of all ages and skill levels.

But that's enough about me for now, let's dive into the book.

# MY TIPS AND TRICKS FOR THE BEST BAKES

## 1
### STAND MIXERS AND ELECTRIC HAND MIXERS

I use an electric hand mixer throughout the book, especially when whipping cream and making cheesecakes, as it's very convenient and can make a big difference to the time and consistency in certain recipes. You do not need an expensive one, I used a £12 hand mixer for years before it finally gave up on me, but it did the job just fine.

I do not use a stand mixer in this book, as I'm aware not a lot of people own one. If you do own one, feel free to use it. Just make sure you keep a close eye on your mixtures so you don't overmix.

## 2
### BALLOON WHISK

To avoid confusion, this is just another name for a standard hand whisk. It's called a balloon whisk because of its shape.

## 3
### SALTED VS UNSALTED BUTTER

You will see in some recipes that I give the option to use salted or unsalted butter. The only thing this will change in these particular recipes is the taste. If you prefer your bakes to be slightly saltier (as I do), feel free to use salted butter. The recipes where I specify unsalted butter generally have salt in the ingredients list already, because I want to control the amount that goes into them.

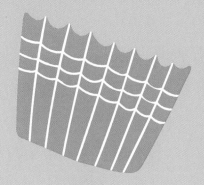

## 4

# USING GRAMS VS CUPS

Baking is a science and accuracy is one of the keys to perfect texture and taste. I always recommend using a set of scales over using cups, as it's more accurate and leaves less room for error, but I do give you cup measurements in this book as well, in case you don't own a set of scales.

## 5

# FOOD COLOURING

When using food colouring, I would strongly recommend using a high-quality brand, such as Sugarflair or Wilton. Supermarket food colourings are generally not strong enough, and using too much to get your desired colour can ruin the consistency of the bake. When adding food colouring to chocolate it's best to use a powdered or oil-based food colouring, rather than a water-based one, as this can make your chocolate seize (when moisture gets into melting chocolate it seizes into a thick, lumpy mixture that you can't use).

## 6

# CHILLING TIMES

I specify chilling times and setting times throughout the book and it's important to stick to these for best results. Cheesecake especially, if not set properly, can collapse if removed from the baking tin too early.

# HOW TO...
## MY MOST-ASKED QUESTIONS

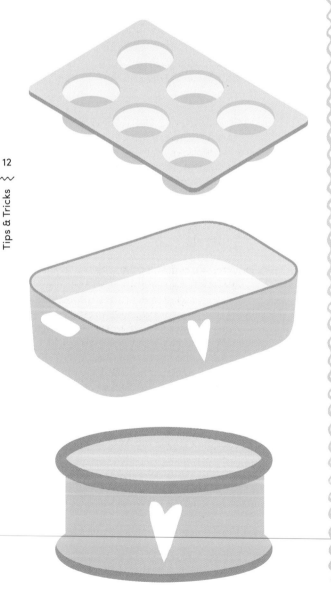

## ... Line your tins

This is one of the things that I get asked the most on social media: how do I line my tins and what baking paper do I use? My favourite is Bacofoil Non-Stick Baking Paper, as it's really thick and holds its shape, and this is how I use it:

- **To line your square or rectangular baking tins,** use two tins of the same size. Measure a piece of baking paper over one of the tins so it has about a 10cm (4in) overhang all the way around the edge. Using the second tin, press the baking paper down into the first tin, then fold the overhang down over the edges, making sure to create sharp creases in the tin so the lining paper holds its shape and is a really snug fit.

- **Lining the bottom of round springform cake tins makes it easier to remove your cooled or chilled bakes.** To do this, place a sheet of baking paper on a chopping board or similar, then place the base of your cake tin on top. With the tip of a sharp knife, 'draw' around the cake tin – you should cut through the paper just enough so that you can press out the circle. Alternatively, grab a pencil and trace around the outside of your cake tin, then cut along the inside line with scissors.

- **The best way to remove a cake or cheesecake from the tin** is to run a sharp knife carefully around the inside of the tin, then unclip it, open the ring and slowly lift it over the cake. Now remove the cake or cheesecake from the tin base, peeling off the lining paper.

## ... Heat a knife

Some of these recipes will recommend you to warm a knife for the best cut.

The best way to do this is to fill a tall, sturdy, heat-proof glass or jug with hot water (enough to cover the blade), then place the knife in the water for a couple of minutes before using.

## ... Melt chocolate

First, break the chocolate into about 1cm (½in) pieces.

- **In the microwave.** Put the chocolate pieces into a microwave-safe bowl and microwave on medium–high in 30–40-second bursts, stirring at each interval. When the chocolate has almost fully melted, continue to stir it with a spoon until all the lumps have disappeared and the chocolate is runny and smooth.

- **In a double boiler**. Make sure you have a saucepan and a large heatproof bowl (I recommend glass) that sits about halfway into your pan. Fill the saucepan with about 5cm (2in) of water. Put your chocolate pieces in the bowl, then sit it on top of the saucepan and turn on the heat so the water starts to simmer. As the water heats up and steam is released, the steam stays trapped between the bowl and the pan, which then heats and melts the chocolate. As this happens, gently stir the chocolate until it's runny and smooth.

## ... Heat-treat flour

When using flour in no-bake recipes and some microwave recipes, it's best to heat-treat the flour first. This is because raw flour can contain bacteria that may be harmful. Better to be safe than sorry...

- **In the microwave.** Put the flour onto a microwave-safe plate and microwave on medium–high for about 90 seconds, stirring every 20 seconds, until the flour is hot throughout. Leave to cool to room temperature before use.

- **In a pan.** Put the flour into a heavy frying pan and warm over a medium heat for 4–4½ minutes, stirring to ensure the flour doesn't burn on the bottom of the pan, until it is hot throughout. Leave to cool to room temperature before use.

# ... Temper chocolate

Why should you temper chocolate?

Tempered chocolate sets hard at room temperature, with a glossy finish and hard snap, meaning it's great when making chocolate bark and truffles, so you can bag them up and give them as gifts. Tempering is also known as pre-crystallising.

You don't have to temper the chocolate in these recipes, but I would recommended it for the perfect finish, and it's really easy to do.

- **In the microwave.** Using the microwave to temper chocolate is one of the best and easiest ways when you only need to temper a small amount of chocolate, as we do in this book.

  01  Break or chop the chocolate into small pieces and put them in a large microwave-safe bowl. I prefer to use a glass bowl.

  02  Microwave on high in short bursts of 15–20 seconds, stirring really well at each interval to make sure the heat is evenly distributed throughout and to stop the chocolate from burning.

  03  Repeat this until almost all of the chocolate has melted, with a few lumps of chocolate left.

  04  Remove the bowl from the microwave and continue to stir the chocolate until there are no lumps left. It should look smooth and slightly thicker.

- **In a double boiler.**

  01  Make sure you have a saucepan and a large heatproof bowl (I recommend glass) that sits about halfway into your pan. Fill the saucepan with about 5cm (2in) of water.

  02  Break or chop the chocolate into small pieces and put three quarters into the glass bowl. Sit it on top of the saucepan and turn on the heat so the water starts to simmer. Heat the chocolate, stirring frequently until it's fully melted.

  03  Remove the bowl from the heat, then add the remaining chopped chocolate (feel free to chop this chocolate up even finer), stirring it in until no lumps remain. The chocolate should be smooth and slightly thicker.

When fully melted, dark chocolate and milk chocolate should be 31–32°C (87.8–89.6°F) and white chocolate should be 29°C (84.2°F), when tested with a cook's thermometer.

To test if the chocolate is tempered properly, dip a knife into the chocolate, then set it aside at room temperature for about 1 minute. If the chocolate hardens, it's done. The chocolate will fully crystallise/temper after 12 hours.

# TRUFFLES and SMALL BITES

# FUN & EASY TO MAKE

This chapter is packed with fun, easy-to-make truffles, fudges and even cookies (yes, oven-less cookies!).

Most of these recipes use just a few ingredients, which are easy to find at your local supermarket, such as chocolate, cream cheese and condensed milk. These recipes are some of my favourites, as they're super simple and a great place to start if you're a beginner baker. There's something so satisfying about just throwing things in a bowl or a pan and creating a delicious dessert out of them.

These recipes are perfect for bringing to parties and sharing with friends and family, or when you just want something sweet and small that doesn't require a fork or a spoon.

If you've been following me on social media for a while, you will know how much I love making fudge. There are so many variations and it always tastes amazing. Be sure to try the Vanilla Honey Fudge on page 32 (you won't find this recipe on my social media, it's exclusive to this book... sshh).

## HERE ARE SOME OF MY TOP TIPS FOR THIS CHAPTER:

- ♥ **Chocolate in fudge:** I tend to use a basic white chocolate as the base in all my fudge recipes, as it's subtle in flavour and allows the other ingredients to shine through. You can use other chocolates such as milk chocolate or dark chocolate, but please be aware this will change the texture and taste of the fudge, and not all fancy chocolates work well. If using dark or milk chocolate, I recommend reducing the amount by 50g (1.75oz).
- ♥ **Heat:** Keep an eye on the heat of your saucepan and don't stop stirring. You're better off starting too low than too high.
- ♥ **Condensed milk:** When using condensed milk in any of my recipes, make sure it's always full-fat, sweetened condensed milk, not the light version or evaporated milk, as this can stop the recipes from setting properly.

Yum!

# SPECULOOS TRUFFLES

## *Makes 10*

These little truffles are perfect if you love a speculoos and white chocolate combo!
And for when you fancy something sweet with the flavours of a speculoos cheesecake,
but don't want to spend long in the kitchen.

**15 minutes**
*+ 1 hour chilling*

100g (3.5oz) speculoos biscuits
60g (4 tbsp) full-fat cream
   cheese, at room temperature
40g (3 tbsp) speculoos spread/
   cookie butter + 20g (1½ tbsp),
   melted, for the drizzle (I use
   Biscoff)
150g (5.25oz) white chocolate,
   broken into pieces

01    Put the biscuits into a food processor and process until finely crushed. Alternatively, put them into a plastic bag and crush with a rolling pin. Tip the crushed biscuits into a medium bowl.

02    Add the cream cheese and the 40g (3 tablespoons) of speculoos spread (cookie butter) and mix in with a spoon until fully combined.

03    Scoop up about 1 tablespoon of the mixture, then roll into a ball with your hands and place on a freezer-proof plate. Repeat with the remaining mixture to make 10 truffles, then transfer to the freezer and chill for 30 minutes.

04    When ready to coat, set a sheet of baking paper over a large plate or tray, then melt the chocolate (see page 13).

05    Using 2 forks, coat each ball in the melted chocolate, letting any excess drip off, then transfer to the prepared plate or tray and drizzle the melted speculoos spread over the top using a piping bag, spoon or fork.

06    Chill in the refrigerator for 30 minutes, or until set. Carefully remove the truffles from the baking paper and serve. Enjoy!

07    Store in an airtight container in the refrigerator for up to 4 days.

# PEANUT BUTTER TRUFFLES

## Makes 20

Think peanut butter cups, but in truffle form. They're sweet, peanut buttery and chocolatey. A peanut butter lover's dream, and they're so easy to make.

### 15 minutes
### + 1 hour chilling

45g (1.5oz) digestive biscuits (or graham crackers)

125g (generous 1 cup) icing (powdered) sugar

60g (4 tbsp) unsalted butter, melted

115g (scant ½ cup) smooth and creamy peanut butter + 50g (5 tbsp) for coating + 20g (2 tbsp) for the drizzle

150g (5.25oz) milk chocolate, broken into pieces

01  Put the biscuits into a food processor and process until finely crushed. Alternatively, put them into a plastic bag and crush with a rolling pin. Tip the crushed biscuits into a medium bowl.

02  Add the icing (powdered) sugar and melted butter and mix in with a spoon until fully combined. Then add the 115g (scant ½ cup) of peanut butter and mix until combined.

03  Scoop up about 1 tablespoon of the mixture, then roll into a ball with your hands and place on a freezer-proof plate. Repeat with the remaining mixture to make 20 truffles, then transfer to the freezer and chill for 30 minutes.

04  When ready to coat, set a sheet of baking paper over a large plate or tray, then melt the chocolate and the 50g (5 tablespoons) of peanut butter together in the same bowl (see page 13).

05  Using 2 forks, coat each ball in the melted chocolate peanut butter mix, letting any excess drip off, then transfer to the prepared plate or tray and drizzle with the remaining peanut butter using a piping bag, spoon or fork.

06  Chill in the refrigerator for 30 minutes, or until set. Carefully remove the truffles from the baking paper and serve. Enjoy!

07  Store in an airtight container in the refrigerator for up to 4 days.

# WHITE CHOCOLATE CHEESECAKE TRUFFLES

## Makes 7

If you love white chocolate cheesecake, these little truffles are for you. They're sweet and creamy and perfect for when you want the delicious taste of a cheesecake without the extra ingredients and extra time in the kitchen.

### 15 minutes
### + 1 hour chilling

80g (2.75oz) shortcake biscuits
60g (4 tbsp) full-fat cream
    cheese, at room temperature
50g (6½ tbsp) icing (powdered)
    sugar
170g (6oz) white chocolate,
    broken into pieces

01  Put the biscuits into a food processor and process until finely crushed. Alternatively, put them into a plastic bag and crush with a rolling pin. Tip the crushed biscuits into a medium bowl.

02  Add the cream cheese and icing (powdered) sugar and mix with a spoon until fully combined.

03  Scoop up about 1 tablespoon of the mixture, then roll into a ball with your hands and place on a freezer-proof plate. Repeat with the remaining mixture to make 7 truffles, then transfer to the freezer and chill for 30 minutes.

04  When ready to coat, set a sheet of baking paper over a large plate or tray, then melt the chocolate (see page 13).

05  Using 2 forks, coat each ball in the melted chocolate, letting any excess drip off, then transfer to the prepared plate or tray and drizzle any remaining melted chocolate over the top using a piping bag, spoon or fork.

06  Chill in the refrigerator for 30 minutes, or until set. Carefully remove the truffles from the baking paper and serve. Enjoy!

07  Store in an airtight container in the refrigerator for up to 4 days.

# EDIBLE COOKIE DOUGH

## Makes about 30 balls

If you think cookie dough is better than the actual cookie itself, I got you.
This cookie dough is so quick and easy to make in just 5 minutes and it's perfect
to use in other no-bake desserts, such as cheesecakes, ice cream (see page 82) or
as cake decorations. You could also roll it into little balls and coat them in chocolate!

### 5 minutes

55g (3½ tbsp) unsalted butter,
  softened
25g (1½ tbsp) granulated sugar
50g (¼ cup) light brown sugar
1 tbsp whole or semi-skimmed
  milk
½ tsp vanilla extract
75g (⅔ cup) plain (all-purpose)
  flour, heat-treated (see page 13)
½ tsp salt
70g (5 tbsp) chocolate chips

01  Put the softened butter and both sugars into a medium mixing
    bowl and cream together using a spoon.

02  Add the milk and vanilla extract and mix until combined. Then
    add the flour and salt and fold in until there are no streaks of
    flour left. Fold in the chocolate chips until evenly distributed.

03  Your cookie dough is now ready to eat or use however you
    wish. My recommendation is to roll it into small balls and store
    in the freezer. You can add it to ice cream, cheesecakes and
    other no-bake desserts; you can also use it as cake decorations.

04  Store in an airtight container in the refrigerator for up to 4 days
    or store in the freezer for up to 3 months.

# CHOCOLATE HAZELNUT FUDGE

## Makes 64 pieces

Calling all chocolate lovers! This fudge is so creamy and chocolatey, quick and easy to make with only 2 ingredients and just 10 minutes prep. Perfect if you're short on time or just want to have some fun in the kitchen.

**10 minutes**
+ 1 hour chilling

500g (1lb) milk chocolate, broken into pieces
420g (1½ cups) chocolate hazelnut spread (I use Nutella), at room temperature

01  Line a 20cm (8in) square tin with nonstick baking paper.

02  Place the milk chocolate into a medium microwave-safe bowl and microwave on medium in 1-minute bursts until melted, then stir gently until smooth.

03  Add the chocolate hazelnut spread and stir in until fully combined.

04  Pour it into your prepared tin and level it out if needed, then chill in the refrigerator for at least 1 hour, or until set.

05  Remove from the refrigerator for around 5–10 minutes before cutting into 64 x 2.5cm (1in) squares.

06  Store in an airtight container in the refrigerator for up to 5 days.

FIVE OR LESS · 5 · FIVE OR LESS

# PEANUT CARAMEL FUDGE

## Makes 64 pieces

This fudge is sweet, caramel-y and nutty. If you love peanuts and caramel, this fudge is for you. It's super quick and easy to make with just 3 ingredients and it's perfect to bring to parties or keep in the fridge for a delicious dessert after dinner.

### 10 minutes
### + 3-4 hours chilling

1 x 397g (14oz) can ready-made caramel (I use Carnation)
500g (1lb) white chocolate, broken into pieces
300g (10.5oz) caramel peanut chocolate bars (I use Snickers), chopped into small slices

Truffles & Small Bites

01   Line a 20cm (8in) square baking tin with nonstick baking paper.

02   Put the caramel and white chocolate into a large saucepan and warm over a low–medium heat, stirring constantly with a wooden spoon or rubber spatula, until the chocolate has melted and the mixture is thick and smooth. It should peel away from the bottom and sides of the pan when you stir the mixture or tilt the pan. If it still looks runny, continue to cook until it thickens.

03   Turn off the heat and add the sliced caramel peanut chocolate bars, reserving around 12–15 slices for the top. Fold in just a few times to avoid completely melting the chocolate, then pour the mixture into your prepared tin and smooth it out to the edges. Press the reserved chocolate slices into the top of the fudge.

04   Chill in the refrigerator for 3–4 hours until set, then cut into 64 x 2.5cm (1in) squares. Enjoy!

05   Store in an airtight container in the refrigerator for up to 5 days.

# VANILLA HONEY FUDGE

## Makes 64 pieces

Vanilla and honey just make the perfect flavour combination. This fudge is one of my favourites in this book. It's sweet and subtle with the ideal fudgy texture; you'll definitely be wanting to make it more than once.

### 10 minutes
### + 3-4 hours chilling

1 x 397g (14oz) can condensed milk
120g (8½ tbsp) unsalted butter
250g (1¼ cups) granulated sugar
30ml (2 tbsp) honey
270g (9.5oz) white chocolate, broken into pieces
2 tsp vanilla extract

01   Line a 20cm (8in) square baking tin with nonstick baking paper.

02   Put the condensed milk, butter, sugar and honey into a large saucepan and warm over a low–medium heat, stirring constantly with a wooden spoon or rubber spatula until everything has melted and the sugar has dissolved. Turn up the heat to medium–high and continue to stir until the mixture bubbles constantly and thickens.

03   Add the white chocolate and vanilla and stir continuously until the chocolate has melted and the mixture is thick and smooth. It should peel away from the bottom and sides of the pan when you stir the mixture or tilt the pan. If it still looks runny, continue to cook until it thickens.

04   Pour the mixture into your prepared tin and smooth it out to the edges, then chill in the refrigerator for 3–4 hours until set. Cut into 64 x 2.5cm (1in) squares and enjoy!

05   Store in an airtight container in the refrigerator for up to 5 days.

# CHOCOLATE OAT COOKIES

## Makes 15

I'm a huge fan of oaty cookies, they have so much texture for the perfect bite. These cookies are packed with peanut butter and chocolate flavours and they taste amazing.

### 10 minutes
### + 30 minutes setting

60g (4 tbsp) salted butter
200g (1 cup) granulated sugar
60ml (¼ cup) whole or semi-
  skimmed milk
15g (2 tbsp) cocoa powder
60g (6 tbsp) smooth and creamy
  peanut butter
2 tsp vanilla extract
125g (1⅓ cups) rolled oats

01   Put the butter, sugar, milk and cocoa powder into a medium saucepan. Stirring frequently, bring the mixture to a boil, then let it boil constantly for 1 minute without stirring.

02   Turn off the heat, then add the peanut butter and vanilla extract and stir until smooth, then fold in the oats until completely coated.

03   Lay down a large piece of nonstick baking paper. Scoop up 2 tablespoons of the mix and drop them onto the paper. You should have 15 cookies in total. Flatten them into circles, then leave to set for 30 minutes at room temperature.

04   Store in an airtight container at room temperature for up to 3 days.

# BREAKFAST COOKIES

## Makes 15

If you love peanut butter as much as I do, you will love these super-easy cookies. They're sweet and nutty, packed with oats and chocolate chips. You can also change up the flavours by adding in chopped nuts or dried fruit to make them your own.

**5 minutes**
**+ 40 minutes chilling**

180g (2¼ cups) rolled oats
250g (1 cup) smooth and creamy peanut butter
70ml (4½ tbsp) honey
50g (3½ tbsp) chocolate chips or add-ins of your choice, such as chopped nuts or dried fruit

01 Line a baking tray or large plate with nonstick baking paper.

02 Put the oats, peanut butter and honey into a large mixing bowl and mix together with a spoon or rubber spatula until fully combined. Then fold through the chocolate chips or add-ins of your choice.

03 Scoop up approximately 2 tablespoons of the mix and roll it into a ball. Repeat to make 15 balls, then flatten them into cookies on the baking paper.

04 Chill in the refrigerator for at least 40 minutes and serve cold. Enjoy!

05 Store in an airtight container in the refrigerator for up to 1 week.

# CHEESECAKES

# SHOWSTOPPERS!

I just had to dedicate an entire chapter to cheesecakes in this book.

When I think no-bake I instantly think of cheesecakes and there are so many cheesecakes I wanted to put in this book, I think they deserve their own chapter.

I've included some fan favourites in here, such as the Chocolate Crunch Cheesecake on page 42 and the Milk and White Chocolate Cheesecake on page 56, plus some new ones, which I know you'll love such as Salted Caramel Cheesecake (page 49) and Lemon-Blueberry Mini Cheesecakes (page 62).

There are lots of variations of cheesecakes in here, from the large round cheesecakes you probably picture in your head, to cheesecake bars, mini individual cheesecakes and layered cheesecakes served in a jar.

Whether you prefer a chocolatey cheesecake, a fruity one or something that's a total showstopper, you will find it in this chapter. Make sure to also check out the seasonal chapter (pages 222–247) where you'll find even more.

## HERE ARE SOME OF MY TOP TIPS FOR MAKING CHEESECAKES:

- **Cream cheese:** Use good-quality full-fat cream cheese that is thick and creamy (I use Philadelphia) and pour off any excess liquid before using, as this will help the cheesecake to set properly. When making cheesecakes, make sure your cream cheese is at room temperature, as this will help the ingredients to blend more easily, creating a firmer cheesecake.
- **Double cream:** It's important when whipping double cream that it's cold, as warm cream will not whip well. You can also chill your bowl and beaters in the refrigerator to speed things up and help the cream stay cool for longer. Double cream is very popular in the UK, but I'm aware not all countries have it. Look for a cream with a fat percentage of at least 30%. Heavy cream and whipping cream are good alternatives.
- **Chilling times:** The time needed to chill a particular recipe in the refrigerator is always a guide. I give a minimum time to ensure everything is set, but you always have the option to chill overnight.
- **Adding the topping:** If you're adding a heavy topping to your cheesecake, such as chocolate ganache or a spread, make sure the filling has fully set and is firm, otherwise you will end up with a collapsing cheesecake. I always advise putting back in the fridge to let it set again before you decorate and serve.
- **Gelatine:** I prefer not to use gelatine in my no-bake cheesecakes, but you can always add it if this is something you prefer. The key to a perfectly set no-bake cheesecake is ensuring your mixture is as thick and fluffy as possible before it goes into the tin. This is achieved by using the correct ingredients with little water content and not overmixing.

Wow!

# CHOCOLATE CRUNCH CHEESECAKE

## Serves 12
~~

This cheesecake is such a showstopper and it's one of my most popular cheesecakes on social media. It has a buttery biscuit base, a creamy chocolate cheesecake filling, topped with a rich chocolate ganache and encased in chocolate wafer fingers. Feel free to use any flavour of wafer fingers you like to make it your own.

### 20 minutes
+ 6 hours chilling

**FOR THE BASE:**

34 chocolate-covered wafer fingers (you can use milk, white or dark chocolate or a mixture; I use KitKats)
300g (10.5oz) digestive biscuits (or graham crackers)
150g (5.25oz) salted or unsalted butter, melted

**FOR THE FILLING:**

450ml (scant 2 cups) cold double (or heavy) cream
500g (1lb) full-fat cream cheese, at room temperature
120g (1 cup) icing (powdered) sugar
200g (7oz) milk chocolate, melted and cooled slightly

**FOR THE TOPPING:**

100g (3.5oz) dark chocolate, broken into pieces
100ml (scant ½ cup) double (or heavy) cream
6 chocolate-covered wafer fingers, broken into small pieces

**FOR THE BASE:**

01 Line the bottom of a 20cm (8in) round springform cake tin with a circle of nonstick baking paper.

02 Place the chocolate-covered wafer fingers around the inside edge of the prepared tin with the branding facing outwards. The edge of each finger should line up with the neighbouring finger. If there is a small gap at the end, carefully slice a finger in half vertically to fill the gap.

03 Put the biscuits into a food processor and process until finely crushed. Alternatively, put them into a plastic bag and crush with a rolling pin. Tip into a large mixing bowl, then pour in the melted butter and mix with a spoon until fully combined. Carefully scoop the mixture into the tin, making sure you don't knock any of the chocolate-covered wafer fingers over, then press it down firmly with the back of a spoon (this will secure the wafer fingers in place). Pop into the refrigerator while you make the filling.

**FOR THE FILLING:**

04 In a large mixing bowl, whip the cream with an electric hand mixer until stiff peaks form. In a separate large bowl, beat together the cream cheese and icing (powdered) sugar with the electric mixer until smooth, then pour in your melted milk chocolate and beat until just combined. Fold in the whipped cream with a rubber spatula until just combined.

05 Remove the chilled base from the refrigerator, then spoon in the filling, smoothing it out to the edges of the wafer fingers and pressing it down onto the base to avoid any gaps.

**FOR THE TOPPING:**

06 Put the chocolate pieces and cream into a microwave-safe bowl and microwave on high for 1 minute 20 seconds (the

cream should be warm enough to melt the chocolate without boiling and curdling). Leave to stand for about 2 minutes, then stir until the cream and chocolate start to come together. Continue to stir until smooth and creamy.

07   Pour the topping over the filling and quickly smooth it out to the edges using a metal spatula or the back of a spoon. Sprinkle the broken chocolate-covered wafer pieces evenly over the top and chill in the refrigerator for at least 6 hours, or overnight, if possible, until completely set.

08   Store in the refrigerator for up to 3 days.

# LEMON CHEESECAKE

## Serves 12
~~

This cheesecake is so zesty and refreshing. It has a buttery shortbread base, a creamy lemon cheesecake filling and is decorated with fresh whipped cream and lemon zest. If you love lemony desserts, this is the cheesecake for you.

## 20 minutes
### + 6 hours chilling

### FOR THE BASE:
350g (12.4oz) shortbread biscuits
100g (3.5oz) salted or unsalted butter, melted

### FOR THE FILLING:
350ml (1½ cups) cold double (or heavy) cream
500g (1lb) full-fat cream cheese, at room temperature
120g (1 cup) icing (powdered) sugar
60ml (4 tbsp) lemon juice

### FOR THE TOPPING:
Lemon zest
150ml (⅔ cup) double (or heavy) cream
6 lemon slice halves

### FOR THE BASE:
01 Line the bottom of a 20cm (8in) round springform cake tin with a circle of nonstick baking paper.

02 Put the biscuits into a food processor and process until finely crushed. Alternatively, put them into a plastic bag and crush with a rolling pin. Tip into a large mixing bowl, then pour in the melted butter and mix with a spoon until fully combined. Press the mixture firmly into the bottom of your prepared tin with the back of a spoon, then pop into the refrigerator while you make the filling.

### FOR THE FILLING:
03 In a large mixing bowl, whip the cream with an electric hand mixer until stiff peaks form. In a separate large bowl, beat together the cream cheese, icing (powdered) sugar and lemon juice with the electric mixer until just combined, then fold in the whipped cream with a rubber spatula until just combined. Be careful not to overmix as this can make the cheesecake go runny.

04 Remove the chilled base from the refrigerator, then spoon in the filling, smoothing it out to the edges and pressing it down onto the base to avoid any gaps. Chill in the refrigerator for at least 6 hours, or overnight, if possible, until completely set.

### FOR THE TOPPING:
05 Remove the cheesecake from the tin and transfer onto a serving plate, then sprinkle lemon zest evenly over the top of the cheesecake.

06 Whip the cream to stiff peaks so it's pipeable and holds its shape, then transfer to a piping bag with your favourite nozzle and pipe it around the edge of your cheesecake.

07 Decorate with the lemon slices however you wish, using the photo as a guide, then serve straight away or store in the refrigerator for up to 3 days.

# WHITE CHOCOLATE and RASPBERRY CHEESECAKE

## Serves 12

Raspberry and white chocolate are a perfect flavour combination. The sweet creaminess from the white chocolate paired with the fresh, tart raspberries is a match made in heaven. This cheesecake has a buttery shortbread base, a creamy white chocolate and raspberry cheesecake filling and is topped with a sweet white chocolate ganache, decorated with fresh raspberries.

### 50 minutes
+ 8 hours chilling

### FOR THE BASE:
350g (12.4oz) shortbread biscuits
100g (3.5oz) salted or unsalted
  butter, melted

### FOR THE FILLING:
350ml (1½ cups) cold double
  (or heavy) cream
500g (1lb) full-fat cream cheese,
  at room temperature
120g (1 cup) icing (powdered)
  sugar
250g (9oz) white chocolate,
  melted and cooled slightly
250g (9oz) fresh raspberries

### FOR THE TOPPING:
170g (6oz) white chocolate,
  broken into pieces
90ml (6 tbsp) double (or heavy)
  cream
200g (7oz) fresh raspberries
1–2 tbsp freeze-dried raspberries
  (optional)

### FOR THE BASE:

01  Line the bottom of a 20cm (8in) round springform cake tin with a circle of nonstick baking paper.

02  Put the biscuits into a food processor and process until finely crushed. Alternatively, put them into a plastic bag and crush with a rolling pin. Tip into a large mixing bowl, then pour in the melted butter and mix with a spoon until fully combined. Press the mixture firmly into the bottom of your prepared tin with the back of a spoon, then pop into the refrigerator while you make the filling.

### FOR THE FILLING:

03  In a large mixing bowl, whip the cream with an electric hand mixer until stiff peaks form. In a separate large bowl, beat together the cream cheese and icing (powdered) sugar with the electric mixer until smooth, then pour in your melted white chocolate and beat until just combined. Fold in the whipped cream with a rubber spatula until just combined, then gently fold in the raspberries; try your best not to crush them.

04  Remove the chilled base from the refrigerator, then spoon in the filling, smoothing it out to the edges and pressing it down onto the base to avoid any gaps. Chill in the refrigerator for at least 6 hours, or overnight, if possible, until completely set.

### FOR THE TOPPING:

05  When ready to decorate, put the chocolate pieces and cream into a microwave-safe bowl and microwave on high for 1 minute 20 seconds (the cream should be warm enough to melt the chocolate without boiling and curdling). Leave to stand for about 2 minutes, then stir until the cream and chocolate start to come together. Continue to stir until smooth and creamy. If the ganache is too runny, pop it in the refrigerator for 20 minutes to help it thicken.

06  Remove the cheesecake from the tin and transfer to a wire rack. Pour over the ganache, allowing it to drip over the edge. Quickly smooth the top using a metal spatula or the back of a spoon. Chill in the refrigerator for around 2 hours to set the ganache. Place the fresh and freeze-dried raspberries on top of the cheesecake however you wish; feel free to use the photo as a guide. Cut into 12 slices to serve.

07  Store in the refrigerator for up to 3 days.

# SALTED CARAMEL CHEESECAKE

## Serves 12

Salted caramel is one of my favourite flavours, I love the sweet and saltiness together.
This cheesecake is packed with so many flavours and textures from the buttery biscuit
base to the creamy cheesecake filling and the silky smooth topping. Just perfection.

## 20 minutes
### + 7 hours chilling

**FOR THE BASE:**
300g (10.5oz) digestive biscuits
(or graham crackers)
150g (5.25oz) salted butter,
melted

**FOR THE FILLING:**
250ml (1 cup) cold double
(or heavy) cream
500g (1lb) full-fat cream cheese,
at room temperature
120g (1 cup) icing (powdered)
sugar
100g (3.5oz) thick ready-made
salted caramel sauce (I use
Sainsbury's Taste the Difference
Salted Caramel Sauce)

**FOR THE TOPPING:**
100g (3.5oz) thick ready-made
salted caramel sauce
3 tbsp mini fudge pieces
Sprinkle of flaky sea salt

**FOR THE BASE:**

01  Line the bottom of a 20cm (8in) round springform cake tin with
a circle of nonstick baking paper.

02  Put the biscuits into a food processor and process until finely
crushed. Alternatively, put them into a plastic bag and crush with
a rolling pin. Tip into a large mixing bowl, then pour in the melted
butter and mix with a spoon until fully combined. Press the mixture
firmly into the bottom of your prepared tin with the back of a
spoon, then pop into the refrigerator while you make the filling.

**FOR THE FILLING:**

03  In a large mixing bowl, whip the cream with an electric
hand mixer until stiff peaks form. In a separate large bowl,
beat together the cream cheese, icing (powdered) sugar
and salted caramel sauce with the electric mixer until just
combined, then fold in the whipped cream with a rubber
spatula until just combined. Be careful not to overmix as this
can make the cheesecake go runny.

04  Remove the chilled base from the refrigerator, then spoon in
the filling, smoothing it out to the edges and pressing it down
onto the base to avoid any gaps. Chill in the refrigerator for at
least 6 hours, or overnight, if possible, until completely set.

**FOR THE TOPPING:**

05  Warm the salted caramel sauce in the microwave for 10–20
seconds on medium until it's runny, then leave to cool slightly.

06  Remove the cheesecake from the tin and transfer onto a wire
rack, then carefully pour the salted caramel sauce over the
top, letting it drip over the edges slightly. You may need to do
this a couple of times to get a nice thick layer. Return it to the
refrigerator for around 1 hour, or until the topping has fully set.

07  Remove from the refrigerator and decorate with mini fudge
pieces around the edge and a sprinkle of flaky sea salt all over
the top.

08  Serve straight away or store in the refrigerator for up to 3 days.

FAN FAVOURITE · FAN FAVOURITE ·

# CHOCOLATE HAZELNUT CHEESECAKE

## Serves 12

This cheesecake is so chocolatey and delicious! It has a buttery cookies and cream base, a super-creamy chocolate hazelnut filling and a thick chocolate hazelnut spread topping.

**20 minutes**
+ 7 hours chilling

### FOR THE BASE:
290g (10.25oz) (about 26) cookies and cream biscuits (I use Oreos)
90g (6 tbsp) unsalted or salted butter, melted

### FOR THE FILLING:
400ml (1⅔ cups) cold double (or heavy) cream
500g (1lb) full-fat cream cheese, at room temperature
80g (⅔ cup) icing (powdered) sugar
450g (generous 1½ cups) chocolate hazelnut spread (I use Nutella)

### FOR THE TOPPING:
150g (½ cup) chocolate hazelnut spread
2 tbsp chopped roasted hazelnuts, to decorate

### FOR THE BASE:
01  Line the bottom of a 20cm (8in) round springform cake tin with a circle of nonstick baking paper.

02  Put the biscuits into a food processor and process until finely crushed. Alternatively, put them into a plastic bag and crush with a rolling pin. Tip into a large mixing bowl, then pour in the melted butter and mix with a spoon until fully combined. Press the mixture firmly into the bottom of your prepared tin with the back of a spoon, then pop into the refrigerator while you make the filling.

### FOR THE FILLING:
03  In a large mixing bowl, whip the cream with an electric hand mixer until stiff peaks form. In a separate bowl, beat together the cream cheese, icing (powdered) sugar and chocolate hazelnut spread with the electric mixer to combine, then fold in the whipped cream with a spatula until just combined. Do not overmix as this can make the cheesecake go runny.

04  Remove the chilled base from the refrigerator, then spoon in the filling, smoothing it out to the edges and pressing it down onto the base to avoid any gaps. Chill in the refrigerator for at least 6 hours, or overnight, if possible, until completely set.

### FOR THE TOPPING:
05  Warm the chocolate hazelnut spread in the microwave in 30-second bursts on medium until it's smooth and runny.

06  Remove the cheesecake from the tin and transfer onto a wire rack, then pour the melted chocolate spread on top, smoothing it out quickly and letting it drip over the edges slightly. Return it to the refrigerator for around 1 hour, or until the topping has set.

07  Remove from the refrigerator and decorate with chopped roasted hazelnuts around the edge.

08  Serve straight away or store in the refrigerator for up to 3 days.

# CARAMEL SHORTBREAD CHEESECAKE

## Serves 12

If you love caramel, shortbread and chocolate, this cheesecake has it all and it's definitely a crowd-pleaser. Encased in caramel shortbread fingers, this cheesecake is guaranteed to wow your friends and family.

### 20 minutes
+ 6 hours chilling

### FOR THE BASE:
25½ mini caramel shortbread chocolate bars (I use Twix)
200g (7oz) shortbread biscuits
80g (5½ tbsp) salted or unsalted butter, melted

### FOR THE FILLING:
250ml (1 cup) cold double (or heavy) cream
500g (1lb) full-fat cream cheese, at room temperature
120g (1 cup) icing (powdered) sugar
100g (3.5oz) thick ready-made caramel sauce (I use Sainsbury's Taste the Difference Salted Caramel Sauce)

### FOR THE TOPPING:
120g (4.5oz) thick ready-made caramel sauce, warm, but not hot
120g (4.5oz) milk chocolate, broken into pieces
80ml (⅓ cup) double (or heavy) cream

### FOR THE BASE:

01 Line the bottom of a 20cm (8in) round springform cake tin with a circle of nonstick baking paper.

02 Place the mini caramel shortbread chocolate bars around the inside edge of the prepared tin with the flat side facing inwards. The edges of each chocolate bar should line up next to its neighbours. If there is a small gap at the end, carefully slice a bar in half vertically to fill the gap.

03 Put the biscuits into a food processor and process until finely crushed. Alternatively, put them into a plastic bag and crush with a rolling pin. Tip into a large mixing bowl, then pour in the melted butter and mix with a spoon until fully combined. Carefully scoop the mixture into the tin, making sure you don't knock any of the chocolate bars over, then press it down firmly with the back of a spoon (this will secure the chocolate bars in place). Pop into the refrigerator while you make the filling.

### FOR THE FILLING:

04 In a large mixing bowl, whip the cream with an electric hand mixer until stiff peaks form. In a separate large bowl, beat together the cream cheese and icing (powdered) sugar with the electric mixer until smooth, then add your caramel sauce and mix until just combined. Fold in the whipped cream with a rubber spatula until just combined.

05 Remove the chilled base from the refrigerator, then spoon in the filling, smoothing it out to the edges of the chocolate bars and pressing it down onto the base to avoid any gaps.

### FOR THE TOPPING:

06 Pour the warm caramel sauce over the cheesecake filling and quickly smooth it out to the edges using a metal spatula or the back of a spoon.

07  Put the chocolate pieces and cream into a microwave-safe bowl and microwave on high for 1 minute 20 seconds (the cream should be warm enough to melt the chocolate without boiling and curdling). Leave to stand for about 2 minutes, then stir until the cream and chocolate start to come together. Continue to stir until smooth and creamy.

08  Pour the ganache over the caramel layer, spreading it out quickly yet gently so it creates a smooth, even layer over the top.

09  Chill in the refrigerator for at least 6 hours, or overnight, if possible, until completely set.

10  Store in the refrigerator for up to 3 days.

# PEANUT BUTTER CUP CHEESECAKE

## Serves 12
~~

This is perfect for any peanut butter lover, with a crunchy, buttery cookies and cream base, a peanut butter filling, a rich chocolate ganache topping and lots of peanut butter cups.

### 20 minutes
### + 7 hours chilling

**FOR THE BASE:**
290g (10.25oz) (about 26) cookies and cream biscuits (I use Oreos)
90g (6 tbsp) unsalted or salted butter, melted

**FOR THE FILLING:**
400ml (1⅔ cups) cold double (or heavy) cream
500g (1lb) full-fat cream cheese, at room temperature
100g (generous ¾ cup) icing (powdered) sugar
400g (1½ cups) smooth and creamy peanut butter
150g (5.25oz) mini peanut butter cups (I use Reese's), cut in half

**FOR THE TOPPING:**
150g (5.25oz) milk chocolate, broken into pieces
120ml (½ cup) double (or heavy) cream
150g (5.25oz) mini peanut butter cups, cut in half, to decorate

**FOR THE BASE:**

01 Line the bottom of a 20cm (8in) round springform cake tin with a circle of nonstick baking paper.

02 Put the biscuits into a food processor and process until finely crushed. Alternatively, put them into a plastic bag and crush with a rolling pin. Tip into a large mixing bowl, then pour in the melted butter and mix with a spoon until fully combined. Press the mixture firmly into the bottom of your prepared tin with the back of a spoon, then pop into the refrigerator while you make the filling.

**FOR THE FILLING:**

03 In a large mixing bowl, whip the cream with an electric hand mixer until stiff peaks form. In a separate large bowl, beat together the cream cheese, icing (powdered) sugar and peanut butter with the electric mixer until just combined, then fold in the whipped cream with a rubber spatula until just combined, followed by the halved mini peanut butter cups. Be careful not to overmix as this can make the cheesecake go runny.

04 Remove the chilled base from the refrigerator, then spoon in the filling, smoothing it out to the edges and pressing it down onto the base to avoid any gaps. Chill in the refrigerator for at least 6 hours, or overnight, if possible, until completely set.

**FOR THE TOPPING:**

05 When ready to decorate, put the chocolate pieces and cream into a microwave-safe bowl and microwave on high for 1 minute 20 seconds (the cream should be warm enough to melt the chocolate without boiling and curdling). Leave to stand for about 2 minutes, then stir until the cream and chocolate start to come together. Continue to stir until smooth and creamy.

06 Remove the cheesecake from the tin and transfer to a wire rack, then pour the ganache over the top, spreading it out quickly and allowing it to drip over the edges slightly. Return it to the refrigerator for 1 hour, or until the topping has fully set, then decorate with the halved mini peanut butter cups.

07 Serve straight away or store in the refrigerator for up to 3 days.

# MILK and WHITE CHOCOLATE CHEESECAKE

## Serves 12
~~

This cheesecake has the perfect balance of milk chocolate and white chocolate. It's super creamy with a milky chocolate ganache on top, decorated with whipped cream and chunks of chocolate. If you love creamy desserts, this cheesecake is the perfect choice.

**30 minutes**
**+ 7 hours chilling**

### FOR THE BASE:
350g (12.4oz) digestive biscuits (or graham crackers)
180g (6oz) salted or unsalted butter, melted

### FOR THE FILLING:
400ml (1⅔ cups) cold double (or heavy) cream
500g (1lb) full-fat cream cheese, at room temperature
120g (1 cup) icing (powdered) sugar
200g (7oz) milk and white chocolate bars (I use Kinder), melted and cooled slightly

### FOR THE TOPPING:
200g (7oz) milk and white chocolate bars (I use Kinder), broken into pieces
120ml (½ cup) double (or heavy) cream + 150ml (⅔ cup) cold double (or heavy) cream for whipping
4 mini milk and white chocolate bars (I use Kinder), cut into pieces, to decorate

### FOR THE BASE:

01   Line the bottom of a 20cm (8in) round springform cake tin with a circle of nonstick baking paper.

02   Put the biscuits into a food processor and process until finely crushed. Alternatively, put them into a plastic bag and crush with a rolling pin. Tip into a large mixing bowl, then pour in the melted butter and mix with a spoon until fully combined. Press the mixture firmly into the bottom of your prepared tin with the back of a spoon, then pop into the refrigerator while you make the filling.

### FOR THE FILLING:

03   In a large mixing bowl, whip the cream with an electric hand mixer until stiff peaks form. In a separate large bowl, beat together the cream cheese, icing (powdered) sugar and melted chocolate with the electric mixer until just combined, then fold in the whipped cream with a rubber spatula until just combined. Be careful not to overmix as this can make the cheesecake go runny.

04   Remove the chilled base from the refrigerator, then spoon in the filling, smoothing it out to the edges and pressing it down onto the base to avoid any gaps. Chill in the refrigerator for at least 6 hours, or overnight, if possible, until completely set.

### FOR THE TOPPING:

05   When ready to decorate, put the chocolate pieces and 120ml (½ cup) of cream into a microwave-safe bowl and microwave on high for 1 minute 20 seconds (the cream should be warm enough to melt the chocolate without boiling and curdling). Leave to stand for about 2 minutes, then stir until the cream and chocolate start to come together. Continue to stir until smooth and creamy, then leave to cool until lukewarm to touch but still pourable.

06   Remove the cheesecake from the tin and transfer to a wire rack, then pour the ganache over the top, spreading it out

quickly and allowing it to drip over the edges slightly. Return it
to the refrigerator for 1 hour, or until the topping has fully set.

07   Whip the 150ml (⅔ cup) of cold cream to stiff peaks using an
     electric hand mixer and transfer into a piping bag with your
     favourite piping nozzle, then pipe it around the edge of the
     cheesecake and decorate with the mini chocolate bar pieces.
     See the photo for inspiration.

08   Serve straight away or store in the refrigerator for up to 3 days.

# CHOCOLATE CHIP COOKIE MINI CHEESECAKES

## *Makes 9*

Think cupcakes, but in cheesecake form. If you love chocolate chip cookies, these are the perfect cheesecakes for you. They have a buttery chocolate chip cookie base, with a creamy chocolate chip cheesecake filling, topped with whipped cream, more chocolate chips and half a cookie. Yum!

**20 minutes**
+ 3 hours chilling

### FOR THE BASE:
150g (5.25oz) crunchy chocolate chip cookies (I use Maryland cookies)
60g (4 tbsp) salted or unsalted butter, melted

### FOR THE FILLING:
250ml (1 cup) cold double (or heavy) cream
350g (2¾ cups) full-fat cream cheese, at room temperature
120g (1 cup) icing (powdered) sugar
70g (5 tbsp) milk or dark chocolate chips

### TO DECORATE:
200ml (scant 1 cup) cold double (or heavy) cream
50g (3½ tbsp) milk or dark chocolate chips
4½ crunchy chocolate chip cookies, cut in half

### FOR THE BASE:

01  Line a cupcake tray with 9 muffin liners. Alternatively, you can use 7.5cm (3in) mini cheesecake rings.

02  Put the cookies into a food processor and process until finely crushed. Alternatively, put them into a plastic bag and crush with a rolling pin. Tip into a medium mixing bowl, then pour in the melted butter and mix with a spoon until fully combined. Press the mixture firmly into the bottom of your muffin liners or rings with the back of a spoon, then pop in the refrigerator while you make the filling.

### FOR THE FILLING:

03  In a large mixing bowl, whip the cream with an electric hand mixer until stiff peaks form. In a separate large bowl, beat together the cream cheese and icing (powdered) sugar with the electric mixer until just combined, then fold in the whipped cream with a rubber spatula until just combined, followed by the chocolate chips. Be careful not to overmix as this can make the cheesecakes go runny.

04  Remove the chilled bases from the refrigerator, then spoon in the filling, smoothing it out to the edges and pressing it down onto the bases to avoid any gaps. Chill in the refrigerator for at least 3 hours, until completely set.

### TO DECORATE:

05  When ready to decorate, whip the cream to stiff peaks and transfer to a piping bag with your favourite piping nozzle.

06  Pipe the whipped cream onto the cheesecakes, then decorate with chocolate chips and half a cookie, as shown in the photo.

07  Serve straight away or store in the refrigerator for up to 3 days.

# COOKIES and CREAM MINI CHEESECAKES

### Makes 9

Cookies and cream is one of my favourite cheesecake flavours. These mini cheesecakes are so quick and easy to make. They're sweet and creamy with that crunchy biscuit base, perfect for any occasion.

### 20 minutes
+ 3 hours chilling

**FOR THE BASE:**

150g (5.25oz) cookies and cream biscuits (I use Oreos)

45g (3 tbsp) unsalted or salted butter, melted

**FOR THE FILLING:**

250ml (1 cup) cold double (or heavy) cream

350g (2¾ cups) full-fat cream cheese, at room temperature

100g (generous ¾ cup) icing (powdered) sugar

55g (1.75oz) (about 5) cookies and cream biscuits, finely crushed

**TO DECORATE:**

200ml (scant 1 cup) cold double (or heavy) cream

2 cookies and cream biscuits, finely crushed

4½ cookies and cream biscuits, cut in half

**FOR THE BASE:**

01  Line a cupcake tray with 9 muffin liners. Alternatively, you can use 7.5cm (3in) mini cheesecake rings.

02  Put the biscuits into a food processor and process until finely crushed. Alternatively, put them into a plastic bag and crush with a rolling pin. Tip into a medium mixing bowl, then pour in the melted butter and mix with a spoon until fully combined. Press the mixture firmly into the bottom of your muffin liners or rings with the back of a spoon, then pop in the refrigerator while you make the filling.

**FOR THE FILLING:**

03  In a large mixing bowl, whip the cream with an electric hand mixer until stiff peaks form. In a separate large bowl, beat together the cream cheese and icing (powdered) sugar with the electric mixer until just combined, then fold in the whipped cream with a rubber spatula until just combined, followed by the crushed biscuits. Be careful not to overmix as this can make the cheesecakes go runny.

04  Remove the chilled bases from the refrigerator, then spoon in the filling, smoothing it out to the edges and pressing it down onto the bases to avoid any gaps. Chill in the refrigerator for at least 3 hours, until completely set.

**TO DECORATE:**

05  When ready to decorate, whip the cream to stiff peaks and transfer to a piping bag with your favourite piping nozzle.

06  Pipe the whipped cream onto the cheesecakes, then decorate with the crushed and halved biscuits, as shown in the photo.

07  Serve straight away or store in the refrigerator for up to 3 days.

# LEMON-BLUEBERRY MINI CHEESECAKES

## Makes 12

These are fresh, fruity, zesty and so creamy. With a buttery biscuit base and lemon-blueberry filling, topped with cream, blueberries and lemon zest – perfect for summer.

### 20 minutes
+ cooling + 3 hours chilling

**FOR THE BLUEBERRY SAUCE:**
250g (8.75oz) fresh or frozen
  blueberries
1 tbsp lemon juice
1 tbsp honey

**FOR THE BASE:**
200g (7oz) digestive biscuits
  (or graham crackers)
100g (3.5oz) unsalted or salted
  butter, melted

**FOR THE FILLING:**
250ml (1 cup) cold double
  (or heavy) cream
350g (2¾ cups) full-fat cream
  cheese, at room temperature
120g (1 cup) icing (powdered)
  sugar

**TO DECORATE:**
300ml (1¼ cups) cold double
  (or heavy) cream
Fresh blueberries
Lemon zest

**FOR THE BLUEBERRY SAUCE:**

01  Put the blueberries, lemon juice and honey into a microwave-safe bowl and microwave on medium in 30-second bursts, stirring in between, to form a thick, jam-like sauce. Alternatively, heat the ingredients in a saucepan over a medium heat, stirring constantly, until melted and thickened. Cool completely.

**FOR THE BASE:**

02  While the sauce is cooling, line a cupcake tray with 9 muffin liners. Alternatively, use 7.5cm (3in) mini cheesecake rings.

03  Put the biscuits into a food processor and process until finely crushed. Alternatively, put them into a plastic bag and crush with a rolling pin. Tip into a medium mixing bowl, then add the melted butter and mix until fully combined. Press it firmly into the bottom of your muffin liners or rings with the back of a spoon, then pop in the refrigerator while you make the filling.

**FOR THE FILLING:**

04  In a large mixing bowl, whip the cream with an electric hand mixer until stiff peaks form. In a separate large bowl, beat together the cream cheese and the icing (powdered) sugar until combined, then fold in the cooled blueberry sauce so it creates swirls through the mix. Fold in the whipped cream with a rubber spatula until just combined. Be careful not to overmix as this can make the cheesecakes go runny.

05  Remove the bases from the refrigerator, then add the filling, smoothing it out to the edges and pressing it down to avoid gaps. Chill in the refrigerator for at least 3 hours, until set.

**TO DECORATE:**

06  Whip the cream to stiff peaks and transfer to a piping bag. Pipe the whipped cream onto the cheesecakes, then decorate with fresh blueberries and lemon zest, as shown in the photo.

07  Serve straight away or store in the refrigerator for up to 3 days.

# LAYERED BLACKBERRY CHEESECAKE JARS

## Makes 4
~~

Cheesecake in a jar, eaten with a spoon, what more could you want? These cheesecakes are so fruity and refreshing, layered with a blackberry sauce, creamy vanilla cheesecake and, of course, a buttery biscuit base.

### 40 minutes
+ cooling + 1 hour chilling

### FOR THE BISCUIT LAYER:
60g (2oz) (4) digestive biscuits (or graham crackers)
30g (2 tbsp) unsalted or salted butter, melted

### FOR THE BLACKBERRY SAUCE:
130g (4.75oz) fresh or frozen blackberries
60ml (4 tbsp) water
1 tbsp honey
30g (2 tbsp) granulated sugar

### FOR THE CHEESECAKE LAYER:
100ml (scant ½ cup) cold double (or heavy) cream
100g (3.5oz) full-fat cream cheese, at room temperature
1 tsp vanilla extract
50g (6½ tbsp) icing (powdered) sugar

### FOR THE BISCUIT LAYER:
01  Put the biscuits into a food processor and process until finely crushed. Alternatively, put them into a plastic bag and crush with a rolling pin. Tip into a medium mixing bowl, then pour in the melted butter and mix with a spoon until fully combined.

### FOR THE BLACKBERRY SAUCE:
02  Put 100g (3.5oz) of the blackberries, the water and honey into a medium saucepan and heat over a medium heat, stirring a few times until it starts to boil. Stir in the granulated sugar, then reduce the heat and let the mix simmer for about 10 minutes. Add the remaining blackberries and let the sauce simmer for 5 minutes, then remove from the heat and leave to cool completely. It should be a thick, jam-like consistency once cool.

### FOR THE CHEESECAKE LAYER:
03  In a large mixing bowl, whip the cream with an electric hand mixer until stiff peaks form. In a separate large bowl, beat together the cream cheese, vanilla extract and icing (powdered) sugar with the electric mixer until combined, then fold in the whipped cream with a rubber spatula.

### TO ASSEMBLE:
04  Divide the biscuit mix evenly between 4 glasses or jars and press it down gently to create a base.

05  Split the cheesecake mix in half, then evenly divide one half between the 4 glasses, piping it onto the biscuit base.

06  Split the blackberry sauce in half, then divide one half between the 4 glasses, smoothing it gently on top of the cheesecake layer.

07  Divide the remaining cheesecake mix between the 4 glasses, piping it onto the blackberry layer.

08  Finally, divide the remaining blackberry sauce between the
    4 glasses, spooning it on top of the cheesecake layer to finish.

09  Chill in the refrigerator for 1 hour, then serve and enjoy!

10  Store in the refrigerator for up to 3 days.

# LAYERED SPECULOOS CHEESECAKE GLASSES

## Makes 4

Speculoos cheesecake is always a winner in my home. The sweet, caramelised biscuit taste complements the creamy cheesecake so perfectly and the layers make every bite taste so delicious. Grab a spoon and dig in.

**20 minutes**
+ 1 hour chilling

### FOR THE BISCUIT LAYER:
60g (2oz) speculoos biscuits
25g (1½ tbsp) unsalted or salted
  butter, melted

### FOR THE CHEESECAKE LAYER:
100ml (scant ½ cup) cold double
  (or heavy) cream
100g (3.5oz) full-fat cream
  cheese, at room temperature
1 tsp vanilla extract
50g (6½ tbsp) icing (powdered)
  sugar
30g (2 tbsp) speculoos spread/
  cookie butter (I use Biscoff)

### TO ASSEMBLE:
200g (generous ¾ cup) speculoos
  spread/cookie butter, melted
1 speculoos biscuit, finely crushed,
  to decorate

### FOR THE BISCUIT LAYER:

01  Put the biscuits into a food processor and process until finely crushed. Alternatively, put them into a plastic bag and crush with a rolling pin. Tip into a medium mixing bowl, then pour in the melted butter and mix with a spoon until fully combined.

### FOR THE CHEESECAKE LAYER:

02  In a large mixing bowl, whip the cream with an electric hand mixer until stiff peaks form. In a separate large bowl, beat together the cream cheese, vanilla extract, icing (powdered) sugar and speculoos spread (cookie butter) with the electric mixer until combined, then fold in the whipped cream with a rubber spatula until just combined.

### TO ASSEMBLE:

03  Divide the biscuit mix evenly between the 4 glasses or jars and press it down gently to create a base.

04  Split the cheesecake mix in half, then evenly divide one half between the 4 glasses, piping it on to the biscuit base.

05  Pour or pipe 25g (1½ tbsp) of melted speculoos spread into each glass on top of the cheesecake layer and smooth it out to the edges if needed.

06  Divide the remaining cheesecake mix between the 4 glasses, piping it onto the speculoos spread.

07  Finally, pour or pipe the remaining speculoos spread into each glass on top of the cheesecake layer and sprinkle with the crushed speculoos biscuit for decoration.

08  Chill in the refrigerator for 1 hour, then serve and enjoy!

09  Store in the refrigerator for up to 3 days.

# CHOCOLATE CHIP COOKIE CHEESECAKE BARS

## Makes 16

A delicious combination of chocolate chip cookies and creamy cheesecake. These cheesecake bars are so easy to make with just 4 ingredients. They have a buttery chocolate chip cookie base, a creamy cheesecake filling packed with cookie chunks, topped with a layer of crunchy chocolate chip cookies.

### 15 minutes
+ 4 hours chilling

#### FOR THE BASE:
200g (7oz) crunchy chocolate chip cookies (I use Maryland cookies)
60g (4 tbsp) unsalted or salted butter, melted

#### FOR THE FILLING AND TOPPING:
500g (1lb) full-fat cream cheese, at room temperature
120g (1 cup) icing (powdered) sugar
200g (7oz) crunchy chocolate chip cookies, broken into pieces

#### FOR THE BASE:

01   Line a 20cm (8in) square baking tin with nonstick baking paper.

02   Put the cookies into a food processor and process until finely crushed. Alternatively, put them into a plastic bag and crush with a rolling pin. Tip into a medium mixing bowl, then pour in the melted butter and mix with a spoon until fully combined.

03   Press it firmly into the bottom of your prepared tin with the back of a spoon, then pop into the refrigerator while you make the filling.

#### FOR THE FILLING AND TOPPING:

04   In a large mixing bowl, beat together the cream cheese and icing (powdered) sugar with an electric hand mixer until smooth. Then fold through half the broken cookies until evenly distributed.

05   Remove the chilled base from the refrigerator and spoon on the filling, smoothing it out to the edges, then place an even layer of the remaining broken cookies on top of the cheesecake.

06   Chill in the refrigerator for at least 4 hours, until completely set. Cut into 16 squares and enjoy!

07   Store in the refrigerator for up to 3 days.

# MILLIONAIRE'S CHEESECAKE BARS

## Makes 16

Think millionaire's shortbread, but in cheesecake form. A buttery shortbread base,
a creamy caramel cheesecake filling, topped with a rich chocolate ganache.
Two delicious desserts in one!

### 20 minutes
+ 4 hours chilling

#### FOR THE BASE:
200g (7oz) shortbread biscuits
60g (4 tbsp) unsalted or salted
butter, melted

#### FOR THE FILLING:
500g (1lb) full-fat cream cheese,
at room temperature
100g (generous ¾ cup) icing
(powdered) sugar
100g (3.5oz) ready-made
caramel (I used Carnation)

#### FOR THE TOPPING:
120g (4.5oz) dark chocolate,
broken into pieces
120ml (½ cup) double (or heavy)
cream
2 tbsp gold or bronze sparkly bits,
to decorate (optional)

#### FOR THE BASE:

01  Line a 20cm (8in) square baking tin with nonstick baking paper.

02  Put the biscuits into a food processor and process until finely crushed. Alternatively, put them into a plastic bag and crush with a rolling pin. Tip into a medium mixing bowl, then pour in the melted butter and mix with a spoon until fully combined.

03  Press the mixture firmly into the bottom of your prepared tin with the back of a spoon, then pop into the refrigerator while you make the filling.

#### FOR THE FILLING:

04  In a large mixing bowl, beat together the cream cheese, icing (powdered) sugar and caramel sauce with an electric hand mixer until smooth. Remove the chilled base from the refrigerator, then spoon on the filling, smoothing it out to the edges.

#### FOR THE TOPPING:

05  Put the chocolate pieces and cream into a microwave-safe bowl and microwave on high for 1 minute 20 seconds (the cream should be warm enough to melt the chocolate without boiling and curdling). Leave to stand for about 2 minutes, then gently stir until the cream and chocolate start to come together. Continue to stir until smooth and creamy. Pour the topping over the cheesecake and smooth it out quickly but gently with the back of a metal spoon or a spatula.

06  Sprinkle the sparkly bits over the top for decoration or decorate however you wish.

07  Chill in the refrigerator for at least 4 hours, or overnight, until completely set. Cut into 16 squares and enjoy!

08  Store in the refrigerator for up to 3 days.

ONE TIN · ONE TIN · ONE TIN · ONE TIN ·

# STRAWBERRIES *and* CREAM CHEESECAKE BARS

## *Makes 16*

These cheesecake bars are fresh and fruity and so creamy and delicious. They have a buttery biscuit base, a creamy cheesecake filling packed with strawberries, topped with whipped cream and fresh strawberries. Perfect for a summer barbecue.

### *20 minutes*
### + 4 hours chilling

### FOR THE BASE:
250g (9oz) digestive biscuits (or graham crackers)
100g (3.5oz) unsalted or salted butter, melted

### FOR THE FILLING:
500g (1lb) full-fat cream cheese, at room temperature
150g (1¼ cups) icing (powdered) sugar
1 tsp vanilla extract
Pink food colouring (optional)
100g (3.5oz) fresh strawberries, diced

### FOR THE TOPPING:
200ml (scant 1 cup) cold double (or heavy) cream
8 fresh strawberries, halved, to decorate

### FOR THE BASE:

01  Line a 20cm (8in) square baking tin with nonstick baking paper.

02  Put the biscuits into a food processor and process until finely crushed. Alternatively, put them into a plastic bag and crush with a rolling pin. Tip into a medium mixing bowl, then pour in the melted butter and mix with a spoon until fully combined.

03  Press the mixture firmly into the bottom of your prepared tin with the back of a spoon, then pop into the refrigerator while you make the filling.

### FOR THE FILLING:

04  In a large mixing bowl, beat together the cream cheese, icing (powdered) sugar, vanilla extract and pink food colouring, if using, with an electric hand mixer until smooth, then fold through the diced strawberries.

05  Remove the chilled base from the refrigerator, then spoon on the filling, smoothing it out to the edges.

06  Chill in the refrigerator for at least 4 hours, or overnight, until completely set. Cut into 16 squares.

### FOR THE TOPPING:

07  Whip the cream with an electric hand mixer to stiff peaks. Pipe the whipped cream in a swirl on top of each square. Place half a strawberry into the whipped cream, as shown in the photo, for decoration. (I find it easiest to do the topping after the cheesecake has been cut into squares.)

08  Store in the refrigerator for up to 3 days.

Cheesecakes

# CREAMY and FROZEN DESSERTS

# SOOOO CREAMY!

This is such a fun chapter! It has everything from ice cream to milkshakes to trifles, pies and more. In this chapter you will find lots of fresh, fruity and, of course, creamy desserts. From Lemon Meringue Pie (page 104) and Key Lime Pie (page 102) – one of my faves – to Cookie Dough Ice Cream (page 82) and a Chocolate Trifle (page 114)!

These recipes are perfect for summer, but you'll be wanting to make them all year round. They're great for dinner parties, barbecues and even cosy nights in because, I don't know about you, but I love having a bowl of ice cream curled up on the sofa on a winter evening.

The majority of these recipes are super easy to make and perfect for beginners, with a few that may require slightly more patience, such as the Triple Chocolate Mousse Cake on page 101.

My top tips for this chapter are below, but please also see the top tips for cheesecakes on page 40, as you may need some of them for this chapter too.

## HERE ARE MY TOP TIPS FOR THIS CHAPTER:

♥ **Overmixing:** Overmixing and overwhipping creamy products, such as double (or heavy) cream, can make it split and/or curdle. You're generally better underwhipping than overwhipping.
♥ **Electric mixer:** I would recommend using an electric hand mixer or stand mixer for this chapter, as whipping cream by hand can be a very long and exhausting process.
♥ **Changing the flavours:** Most of these desserts can be adjusted to incorporate the flavours you like. For example, if you don't like strawberries, you can use raspberries or blueberries, and if you don't like speculoos spread (cookie butter), you can use peanut butter or chocolate spread.
♥ **Ice creams:** When serving the ice creams, make sure to let them sit at room temperature for around 10 minutes to make them easier to scoop. The softness of the ice creams will vary depending on the flavours and ingredients used.

So much fun to make!

# FROZEN VANILLA CHEESECAKE

## Serves 10-12

Is it ice cream, is it cheesecake? With all the flavours of a vanilla cheesecake, from the biscuit base to the creamy vanilla filling, it's a cheesecake in ice-cream form. Grab a spoon and a bowl and dig in.

### 10 minutes
+ 6 hours freezing

1 x 397g (14oz) can condensed milk
200g (7oz) full-fat cream cheese
2 tsp vanilla extract
475ml (scant 2 cups) cold double (or heavy) cream
120g (4.5oz) digestive biscuits (or graham crackers), broken into chunks

01  Put the condensed milk, cream cheese and vanilla extract into a large mixing bowl and beat with an electric hand mixer until combined.

02  In a separate large mixing bowl, whip the cream to stiff peaks, then fold into the cream cheese mixture until smooth and creamy.

03  Fold through the biscuit chunks until evenly distributed.

04  Scoop the mixture into a 20cm (8in) square baking tin or a 1.3kg (3lb) loaf tin or freezer-proof container – feel free to line the tin with baking paper if you prefer – then smooth it out evenly with the back of a spoon.

05  Double wrap the entire tin with cling film (plastic wrap), ensuring no moisture can get in, then freeze for at least 6 hours, or overnight if possible.

06  When ready to serve, remove it from the freezer and leave to stand for 5–10 minutes. Unwrap the tin, then dip an ice-cream scoop into hot water (this makes serving slightly easier) and scoop it into bowls.

07  Store in a sealed container in the freezer for up to 2 months.

Feel free to add your own flavours to this recipe, such as cookies and cream biscuits, strawberries or caramel sauce.

# COOKIE MUNCHER ICE-CREAM CAKE

## Serves 16

Did someone say cookies? This ice-cream cake is fun and so easy to make and perfect for parties. It has a buttery cookies and cream base, a creamy vanilla ice-cream filling that's packed with two types of cookies, topped with whipped cream and, of course, more cookies!

**30 minutes**
*+ 6 hours freezing*

### FOR THE BASE:
300g (10.5oz) cookies and cream biscuits (I use Oreos)
95g (6 tbsp) unsalted butter, melted

### FOR THE ICE CREAM:
1 x 397g (14oz) can condensed milk
400ml (1⅔ cups) cold double (or heavy) cream
2 tsp vanilla extract
Blue food colouring
70g (2.5oz) cookies and cream biscuits (I use Oreos), broken into small chunks
70g (2.5oz) crunchy chocolate chip cookies, broken into small chunks

### FOR THE TOPPING:
150ml (⅔ cup) cold double (or heavy) cream
30g (4 tbsp) icing (powdered) sugar
70g (2.5oz) cookies and cream biscuits, halved
70g (2.5oz) crunchy chocolate chip cookies, halved
Edible eyes (optional)

### FOR THE BASE:

01  Line a 20cm (8in) square baking tin with nonstick baking paper.

02  Put the biscuits into a food processor and process until finely crushed. Alternatively, put them into a plastic bag and crush with a rolling pin. Tip into a medium mixing bowl, then pour in the melted butter and mix with a spoon until fully combined.

03  Press the mixture firmly into your prepared tin with the back of a spoon, then pop into the refrigerator and make the filling.

### FOR THE ICE CREAM:

04  Pour the condensed milk, cream, vanilla extract and blue food colouring into a large mixing bowl and beat with an electric hand mixer until soft peaks form, then fold in the broken biscuits and cookies.

05  Remove the base from the refrigerator, then pour the ice-cream mix into the tin and smooth it out using the back of a metal spoon.

06  Double wrap the entire tin with cling film (plastic wrap), ensuring no moisture can get in, then freeze for at least 6 hours, or overnight if possible.

### FOR THE TOPPING:

07  When ready to serve, pour the cream and icing (powdered) sugar into a large mixing bowl and whip to soft peaks. Then spread it evenly over the ice cream.

08  To decorate, place the biscuit and cookie halves on top of the whipped cream and place 2 edible eyes, if using, above the flat edge of the cookie, as shown in the photo.

09  Store in a sealed container (or wrap the tin in cling film) in the freezer for up to 2 months.

FAN FAVOURITE · FAN FAVOURITE

# COOKIE DOUGH
# ICE CREAM

## Serves 10-12

Cookie dough ice cream is one of my all-time favourite flavours. If you're anything like me, you go digging around for all the cookie dough pieces so you can have extra in your scoop. The vanilla ice cream is thick and luscious and it's packed with lots and lots of chocolate chip cookie dough. Maybe even make a double batch of cookie dough just in case some gets 'accidentally' eaten along the way...

**20 minutes**
+ 6 hours freezing

**FOR THE COOKIE DOUGH:**
See page 27

**FOR THE ICE CREAM:**
1 x 397g (14oz) can condensed milk
475ml (scant 2 cups) cold double (or heavy) cream
2 tsp vanilla extract
50g (3½ tbsp) milk or dark chocolate chips

82

Creamy & Frozen Desserts

**FOR THE COOKIE DOUGH:**

01 Start by making the cookie dough (see page 27).

02 Roll the cookie dough into small balls using about 1 teaspoon of dough per ball, then place them on a freezer-proof plate and pop them in the freezer while you make the ice cream.

**FOR THE ICE CREAM:**

03 Pour the condensed milk, cream and vanilla extract into a large mixing bowl and beat with an electric hand mixer until soft peaks form. Then fold in the cookie dough balls and chocolate chips, saving a handful of each for the top.

04 Scoop the mixture into a 20cm (8in) square baking tin or a 1.3kg (3lb) loaf tin or freezer-proof container – feel free to line the tin with baking paper if you prefer – then smooth it out evenly with the back of a spoon.

05 Place the remaining cookie dough balls and chocolate chips on top, then double wrap the entire tin with cling film (plastic wrap), ensuring no moisture can get in, and freeze for at least 6 hours, or overnight if possible.

06 When ready to serve, remove it from the freezer and leave to stand for 5–10 minutes. Unwrap the tin, then dip an ice-cream scoop into hot water (this makes serving slightly easier) and scoop it into bowls.

07 Store in a sealed container in the freezer for up to 2 months.

# ROCKY ROAD ICE CREAM

## Serves 10-12

~~~

The texture of this ice cream is so thick and creamy. It's packed with all the flavours of a rocky road, from the chocolate ice cream to the sweet marshmallows, biscuit chunks and chocolatey chips. Perfect for any time of the year.

**15 minutes**
+ 6 hours freezing

1 x 397g (14oz) can condensed milk
475ml (scant 2 cups) cold double (or heavy) cream
150g (½ cup) chocolate spread
40g (¾ cup) mini marshmallows
100g (3.5oz) digestive biscuits (or graham crackers or biscuits of your choice), broken into chunks
70g (5 tbsp) milk chocolate chips

01  Pour the condensed milk, cream and chocolate spread into a large mixing bowl and beat with an electric hand mixer until thick and creamy. Then fold in the mini marshmallows, biscuit chunks and chocolate chips, saving a handful of each for the top.

02  Scoop the mixture into a 20cm (8in) square baking tin or a 1.3kg (3lb) loaf tin or freezer-proof container – feel free to line the tin with baking paper if you prefer – then smooth it out evenly with the back of a spoon.

03  Scatter the remaining mini marshmallows, biscuit chunks and chocolate chips on top, then double wrap the entire tin with cling film (plastic wrap), ensuring no moisture can get in, and freeze for at least 6 hours, or overnight if possible.

04  When ready to serve, remove the ice cream from the freezer and leave to stand for 5–10 minutes. Unwrap the tin, then dip an ice-cream scoop into hot water (this makes serving slightly easier) and scoop it into bowls.

05  Store in a sealed container in the freezer for up to 2 months.

# CARAMEL NOUGAT ICE CREAM

## Serves 10-12

This ice cream is one of the easiest in the book. It's quick and easy to make with just 3 ingredients, but it definitely doesn't skimp on flavour. It's so caramel-y and creamy, packed with chunks of chewy caramel nougat bars coated in smooth milk chocolate. Feel free to swap the chocolate bars for something similar if you prefer.

**10 minutes**
+ 6 hours freezing

1 x 397g (14oz) can ready-made caramel (I use Carnation)
475ml (scant 2 cups) cold double (or heavy) cream
250g (9oz) caramel nougat chocolate bars (I use Mars), chopped into small pieces

01  Pour the caramel and cream into a large mixing bowl and beat with an electric hand mixer until it forms soft peaks. Then fold in the caramel nougat chocolate bar pieces, saving a few for the top.

02  Scoop the mixture into a 20cm (8in) square baking tin or a 1.3kg (3lb) loaf tin or freezer-proof container – feel free to line the tin with baking paper if you prefer – then smooth it out evenly with the back of a spoon.

03  Place the remaining pieces of the chocolate bar on top, then double wrap the entire tin with cling film (plastic wrap), ensuring no moisture can get in, and freeze for at least 6 hours, or overnight if possible.

04  When ready to serve, remove the ice cream from the freezer and leave to stand for 5–10 minutes. Unwrap the tin, then dip an ice-cream scoop into hot water (this makes serving slightly easier) and scoop it into bowls.

05  Store in a sealed container in the freezer for up to 2 months.

Add a drizzle of caramel sauce to the ice cream when you serve it for extra caramel-y deliciousness!

# STRAWBERRY SHORTCAKE ICE CREAM

## Serves 10-12

I'm telling you now, strawberry jam and ice cream are a dream combo! This ice cream is sweet and creamy, packed with chunks of shortbread, fresh strawberries and swirls of strawberry jam. It's easy to make and perfect for a hot day.

**15 minutes**
+ 6 hours freezing

1 x 397g (14oz) can condensed milk
475ml (scant 2 cups) cold double (or heavy) cream
2 tsp vanilla extract
100g (3.5oz) shortbread biscuits, crushed
200g (7oz) fresh strawberries, sliced into small pieces
150g (½ cup) strawberry jam

01   Pour the condensed milk, cream and vanilla extract into a large mixing bowl and beat with an electric hand mixer until thick and creamy. Then fold in the crushed biscuits and strawberries, saving a handful of each for the top.

02   Scoop one third of the mixture into a 20cm (8in) square baking tin or a 1.3kg (3lb) loaf tin or freezer-proof container – feel free to line the tin with baking paper if you prefer – then smooth it out evenly with the back of a spoon.

03   Drizzle or dollop on about one third of the strawberry jam. Repeat this 2 more times with the remaining ice-cream mix and strawberry jam. Then sprinkle the remaining crushed biscuits and strawberry pieces over the top.

04   Double wrap the entire tin with cling film (plastic wrap), making sure no moisture can get in, and freeze for at least 6 hours, or overnight if possible.

05   When ready to serve, remove it from the freezer and leave to stand for 5–10 minutes. Unwrap the tin, then dip an ice-cream scoop into hot water (this makes serving slightly easier) and scoop it into bowls.

06   Store in a sealed container in the freezer for up to 2 months.

# LEMON ICE CREAM

## Serves 10-12

This ice cream is so zesty and refreshing. It's great for a hot summer day when you want to cool off and enjoy a delicious bowl of ice cream. Perfect for a garden party or barbecue.

**15 minutes**
+ 6 hours freezing

1 x 397g (14oz) can condensed milk
Juice of 4 lemons (about 180ml/ ¾ cup)
Zest of 1 lemon
475ml (scant 2 cups) cold double (or heavy) cream

Creamy & Frozen Desserts

01  Pour the condensed milk, lemon juice and lemon zest into a large mixing bowl and mix with an electric hand mixer until fully combined.

02  In another large mixing bowl, whip the cream to soft peaks; be careful not to overwhip here.

03  Add a couple of spoonfuls of the whipped cream to the condensed milk mixture and mix together to make it lighter and easier to mix with the rest of the whipped cream.

04  Scoop the rest of the whipped cream into the bowl and fold in with a rubber spatula, trying to keep as much air in the mixture as possible.

05  Scoop the mixture into a 20cm (8in) square baking tin or a 1.3kg (3lb) loaf tin or freezer-proof container – feel free to line the tin with baking paper if you prefer – then smooth it out evenly with the back of a spoon.

06  Double wrap the entire tin with cling film (plastic wrap), ensuring no moisture can get in, and freeze for at least 6 hours, or overnight if possible.

07  When ready to serve, remove it from the freezer and leave to stand for 5–10 minutes. Unwrap the tin, then dip an ice-cream scoop into hot water (this makes serving slightly easier) and scoop it into bowls.

08  Store in a sealed container in the freezer for up to 2 months.

# CHOCOLATE SPECULOOS DREAM BARS

## Makes 16

I called these dream bars for no other reason than they're so dreamy! They have a layer of buttery speculoos biscuits for the base, a creamy layer of chocolate hazelnut cheesecake, a layer of speculoos cheesecake, topped with fresh whipped cream and speculoos biscuit crumbs. They have so many delicious flavours, you'll want to make these again and again.

**20 minutes**
+ 4 hours chilling

### FOR THE BASE:
220g (8oz) speculoos biscuits
60g (4 tbsp) unsalted or salted butter, melted

### FOR THE FILLING:
600g (1lb 5oz) full-fat cream cheese, at room temperature
100g (generous ¾ cup) icing (powdered) sugar
50g (2½ tbsp) chocolate hazelnut spread (I use Nutella)
50g (3½ tbsp) speculoos spread/ cookie butter (I use Biscoff)

### FOR THE TOPPING:
200ml (scant 1 cup) cold double (or heavy) cream
30g (4 tbsp) icing (powdered) sugar

### FOR THE BASE:
01  Line a 20cm (8in) square baking tin with nonstick baking paper.

02  Put the biscuits into a food processor and process until finely crushed. Alternatively, put them into a plastic bag and crush with a rolling pin. Tip into a medium mixing bowl, then set aside 2 tablespoons for the topping. Pour in the melted butter and mix with a spoon until fully combined.

03  Press the mixture firmly into your prepared tin with the back of a spoon, then pop into the refrigerator and make the filling.

### FOR THE FILLING:
04  In a large mixing bowl, beat together the cream cheese and icing (powdered) sugar with an electric hand mixer until smooth, then transfer half of the mixture to another medium or large mixing bowl.

05  Add the chocolate hazelnut spread to one half of the mixture and the speculoos spread (cookie butter) to the other half of the mixture and beat them both individually until fully combined.

06  Remove the chilled base from the refrigerator, then spoon on the chocolate hazelnut filling, smoothing it out to the edges. Then scoop on the speculoos filling and smooth this out.

### FOR THE TOPPING:
07  In a large mixing bowl, whip the cream and icing sugar to soft peaks; be careful not to overwhip. Spread it evenly over the speculoos layer. Sprinkle the remaining biscuit crumbs on top.

08  Chill in the refrigerator for at least 4 hours, or overnight, until completely set. Cut into 16 squares and enjoy!

09  Store in the refrigerator for up to 3 days.

# BERRIES and CREAM LASAGNE

## Serves 9

Don't worry I haven't gone crazy and started mixing meat and potatoes with berries and cream... yet. This fresh and fruity dessert has layers of sweet biscuits, whipped cream, strawberries, raspberries, blueberries and strawberry jam. Leave it overnight to bring all the delicious flavours together for the ultimate summer berry dessert.

## 15 minutes
### + 7 hours chilling

About 21 malted milk biscuits
  or similar
400ml (1⅔ cups) cold double
  (or heavy) cream
50g (6½ tbsp) icing (powdered)
  sugar
2 tsp vanilla extract
200g (7oz) fresh strawberries,
  sliced
150g (5.25oz) fresh blueberries
200g (7oz) fresh raspberries
50g (¼ cup) granulated sugar
100g (⅓ cup) strawberry or
  raspberry jam

01 Arrange a layer of half the biscuits in the bottom of a 24cm (9.5in) x 14cm (5.5in) baking tin. This will also work perfectly in a 20cm (8in) square baking tin. If your tin is slightly bigger or slightly smaller, feel free to fill in the gaps with broken biscuits.

02 Put the cream, icing (powdered) sugar and vanilla extract into a large mixing bowl and use an electric hand mixer to whip to soft peaks.

03 In a medium mixing bowl, coat all the berries in the granulated sugar using a spoon.

04 Spread half the whipped cream evenly over the layer of biscuits, then drizzle over half the jam and scatter half the berries on top.

05 Place on another layer of biscuits, then spread the remaining whipped cream over the top and smooth it out evenly. Then drizzle the remaining jam over the top and decorate with the remaining berries.

06 Chill in the refrigerator for at least 7 hours or overnight, so the biscuits soften and all the flavours come together. Serve cold, cut into 9 pieces. Enjoy!

07 Wrap the tin in cling film (plastic wrap) and store in the refrigerator for up to 3 days.

Feel free to line your baking tin if you want to remove the bake as one to cut up, or you can cut it directly in the tin – whichever you find easiest.

Creamy & Frozen Desserts

# BANOFFEE PIE JARS

## Makes 4

~

Banoffee is one of my favourite desserts ever! I love the combination of the crunchy biscuits with the soft banana, the sweet caramel sauce and freshly whipped cream. Just perfection.

*20 minutes*
*+ 1 hour chilling*

### FOR THE BISCUIT LAYER:
60g (2oz) digestive biscuits
  (or graham crackers)
30g (2 tbsp) unsalted or salted
  butter, melted

### FOR THE CREAM LAYER:
150ml (⅔ cup) cold double
  (or heavy) cream
50g (6½ tbsp) icing (powdered)
  sugar
1 tsp vanilla extract

### TO ASSEMBLE:
1 large banana or equivalent,
  sliced into coins
100g (3.5oz) ready-caramel
  sauce (melted if it isn't a runny
  caramel)

### FOR THE BISCUIT LAYER:

01  Put the biscuits into a food processor and process until finely crushed. Alternatively, put them into a plastic bag and crush with a rolling pin. Tip into a medium mixing bowl, then pour in the melted butter and mix with a spoon until fully combined.

### FOR THE CREAM LAYER:

02  In a large mixing bowl, whip the cream, icing (powdered) sugar and vanilla extract with an electric hand mixer until soft peaks form.

### TO ASSEMBLE:

03  Divide the biscuit mix evenly between 4 jars or glasses, saving about 1 heaped tablespoon of the mix to decorate, and press it down gently to create a base.

04  Split the cream layer in half, then evenly divide one half between the 4 jars, piping it on to the biscuit base.

05  Place a layer of banana slices on top of the cream, then drizzle over the caramel sauce, saving about 4 teaspoons of the caramel sauce to decorate.

06  Divide the remaining whipped cream mix between the 4 jars.

07  Decorate the jars with a sprinkle of the remaining biscuit mix, a drizzle of caramel sauce and a slice of banana, if you wish.

08  Chill in the refrigerator for 1 hour for best results or serve straight away. Enjoy!

09  Store in the refrigerator for up to 3 days.

Creamy & Frozen Desserts

# COOKIES and CREAM PIE

## Serves 12

This dessert is 'exactly what it says on the tin'. It has a buttery cookies and cream pie crust, filled with sweet whipped cream that's packed with cookies. It looks and tastes so amazing, no one would know it was made with just a few simple ingredients.

## 30 minutes
### + 2 hours chilling

### FOR THE BASE:
290g (10.25oz) (about 26) cookies and cream biscuits (I use Oreos)
90g (6 tbsp) unsalted or salted butter, melted

### FOR THE FILLING:
650ml (2¾ cups) cold double (or heavy) cream
80g (⅔ cup) icing (powdered) sugar
10 cookies and cream biscuits, a mixture of crushed and broken into quarters

### TO DECORATE:
6 cookies and cream biscuits, halved

### FOR THE BASE:

01   Put the biscuits into a food processor and process until finely crushed. Alternatively, put them into a plastic bag and crush with a rolling pin. Tip into a medium mixing bowl, then pour in the melted butter and mix with a spoon until fully combined.

02   Pour it into a deep, loose-bottomed 22cm (8½in) pie tin, pressing down firmly into the base and around the edges with the back of a spoon to create your pie crust. Pop it in the refrigerator while you make the filling.

### FOR THE FILLING:

03   In a large mixing bowl, whip the cream and icing (powdered) sugar with an electric hand mixer until soft peaks form, then set aside a quarter for the topping. Fold in the crushed and broken biscuits. The cream should turn slightly grey.

04   Remove the base from the refrigerator and scoop in the filling, smoothing it out to the edges so it's level and smooth on top. Pop it back in the refrigerator for at least 2 hours to set.

### TO DECORATE:

05   Remove it from the refrigerator and pipe the remaining whipped cream around the edge. Place the biscuit halves into the cream, spread evenly apart. Slice with a hot knife for a clean cut. Enjoy!

06   Store in the refrigerator for up to 3 days.

Creamy & Frozen Desserts

# TRIPLE CHOCOLATE MOUSSE CAKE

## Serves 16
~~

This recipe requires a little more time and patience than the majority of the recipes in this book, but we love a challenge and the outcome is definitely worth the wait. It has three layers of chocolate mousse – milk, white and dark – with a crunchy cookies and cream base. It's the perfect showstopping dessert for any dinner party.

## 30 minutes
### + 6 hours chilling

### FOR THE BASE:
290g (10.25oz) (about 26) cookies and cream biscuits (I use Oreos)
90g (6 tbsp) unsalted or salted butter, melted

### FOR THE FILLING:
40–45ml (3 tbsp) cold water
18.5g (6 tsp) gelatine
150g (5.25oz) dark chocolate (around 50% cocoa), broken into pieces
1.1 litre (5 cups) cold double (or heavy) cream
150g (5.25oz) milk chocolate, broken into pieces
150g (5.25oz) white chocolate, broken into pieces
2 tsp cocoa powder, for dusting (optional)

### FOR THE BASE:

01 Line and grease the bottom and sides of a 20cm (8in) round springform cake tin with nonstick baking paper.

02 Put the biscuits into a food processor and process until finely crushed. Alternatively, put them into a plastic bag and crush with a rolling pin. Tip into a large mixing bowl, then pour in the melted butter and mix with a spoon until fully combined. Press the mixture firmly into the bottom of your prepared tin with the back of a spoon, then pop into the refrigerator while you make the filling.

### FOR THE FILLING:

03 In a small saucepan, add 1 tablespoon of the water and 2 teaspoons of the gelatine. Leave to stand for 1 minute, then stir over a low heat until dissolved and remove from the heat.

04 Put the dark chocolate and 150ml (⅔ cup) of the cream into a microwave-safe bowl and microwave on medium for 1 minute 20 seconds. Leave to stand for 1 minute, then stir gently until smooth. Add the gelatine mixture to the bowl and stir in, then leave to cool completely.

05 Repeat step 4 with the remaining water, gelatine, the cream and the milk chocolate and then the white chocolate.

06 Beat the remaining cream to soft peaks. Fold one third of it into the dark chocolate mix until smooth and combined and spread over the base. Chill in the refrigerator for 30 minutes until set.

07 Repeat step 6 with the milk chocolate and then the white chocolate, making sure the whipped cream stays cold.

08 Pop it in the refrigerator for at least 5 hours, or until set.

09 When ready to serve, dust with cocoa powder, then remove the ring and baking paper if you wish. Slice with a hot knife for a clean cut and serve cold. Enjoy!

10 Store in the refrigerator for up to 3 days.

# KEY LIME PIE

### Serves 12
~~

Fun fact, Key West (the home of the key lime pie) is where I got married and I have tried many, many key lime pies in Key West. The best ones always have a crunchy, salty base, a creamy, zesty, strong lime filling and are either topped with meringue or whipped cream. I went for whipped cream here to keep it simple, but feel free to top it with a homemade meringue (see page 104).

**25 minutes**
**+ 3 hours chilling**

### FOR THE BASE:
300g (10.5oz) digestive biscuits (or graham crackers)
150g (5.25oz) salted butter, melted

### FOR THE FILLING:
300ml (1¼ cups) cold double (or heavy) cream
1 x 397g (14oz) can condensed milk
180ml (¾ cup) lime juice (roughly 6 limes)
Zest of 3 limes

### FOR THE TOPPING:
150ml (⅔ cup) cold double (or heavy) cream
30g (4 tbsp) icing (powdered) sugar
Zest of 2 limes
Lime wedges, to decorate

### FOR THE BASE:

01 Put the digestive biscuits into a food processor and process until finely crushed. Alternatively, put them into a plastic bag and crush with a rolling pin. Tip into a medium mixing bowl, then pour in the melted butter and mix with a spoon until fully combined.

02 Pour it into a deep, loose-bottomed 22cm (8½in) pie tin, pressing down firmly into the base and around the edges with the back of a spoon to create your pie crust. Pop it in the refrigerator while you make the filling.

### FOR THE FILLING:

03 In a large mixing bowl, whip the cream with an electric hand mixer until stiff peaks form.

04 In another large mixing bowl, beat together the condensed milk, lime juice and lime zest until combined, then fold in the whipped cream.

05 Remove the base from the refrigerator and pour in the filling, smoothing it out so it's level, then chill in the refrigerator for at least 3 hours.

### FOR THE TOPPING:

06 Whip the cream and icing (powdered) sugar to stiff peaks, then remove the pie from the refrigerator and pipe whipped cream around the edge. Sprinkle the lime zest over the top and decorate with lime wedges. Slice with a hot knife for a clean cut. Enjoy!

07 Store in the refrigerator for up to 3 days.

# LEMON MERINGUE PIE

## Serves 12
~~

Lemon meringue pie is the perfect summer dessert, if you ask me. It has a buttery, crunchy crust, a zesty, refreshing filling and a sweet toasted meringue on top. Pure bliss.

## 40 minutes
+ 1 hour cooling and chilling

### FOR THE BASE:
300g (10.5oz) digestive biscuits (or graham crackers)
150g (5.25oz) salted butter, melted

### FOR THE FILLING:
215ml (scant 1 cup) (about 5 lemons) lemon juice
Zest of 3 lemons
280g (scant 1½ cups) granulated sugar
5 egg yolks (save the whites for the meringue)
100ml (scant ½ cup) whole milk
50g (5 tbsp) cornflour (cornstarch)
50g (3½ tbsp) salted butter, cubed

### FOR THE MERINGUE:
140g (¾ cup) granulated sugar
70ml (4 tbsp) water
3 egg whites

### FOR THE BASE:
01 Put the biscuits into a food processor and process until finely crushed. Alternatively, put them into a plastic bag and crush with a rolling pin. Tip into a medium mixing bowl, then pour in the melted butter and mix with a spoon until fully combined.

02 Pour it into a deep, loose-bottomed 22cm (8½in) pie tin, pressing down firmly into the base and around the edges with the back of a spoon. Pop it in the refrigerator while you make the filling.

### FOR THE FILLING:
03 Put the lemon juice, lemon zest, sugar, egg yolks, milk and cornflour (cornstarch) into a large mixing bowl and set over a saucepan of simmering (not boiling) water.

04 Keep whipping until the mixture thickens, then remove the bowl from the heat and beat in the butter until combined.

05 Remove the base from the refrigerator and pour in the filling. Leave to cool completely, then refrigerate for 30 minutes.

### FOR THE MERINGUE:
06 Put the sugar and water into a large, heavy-based saucepan and bring to the boil, gently stirring occasionally.

07 When the sugar reaches 105°C (221°F) – test this with a sugar thermometer – in a large mixing bowl, whip the egg whites to stiff peaks using an electric hand mixer.

08 When the sugar syrup reaches 120°C (248°F), slowly pour it into the egg whites at the edge of the bowl, whipping at the same time. Be sure to do this slowly so the egg whites stay smooth.

09 When all the syrup is in, continue whipping on a high speed for about 5 minutes until the mixture is smooth, glossy and cooled.

### TO DECORATE:
10 Dollop the meringue on top in a mound shape, then use a blowtorch or quickly put it under a hot grill to toast the edges.

11 Store in the refrigerator for up to 3 days.

# SALTED CARAMEL TART

## Serves 16
~~

If you love rich chocolate and sweet, salty caramel, I got you. This tart is the ultimate chocolate indulgence and it's so quick and easy to make. Your taste buds will thank you.

**15 minutes**
+ 4 hours chilling

## FOR THE BASE:
300g (10.5oz) digestive biscuits (or graham crackers)
150g (5.25oz) salted butter, melted
400g (14oz) thick ready-made salted caramel sauce (I use Sainsbury's Taste the Difference Salted Caramel Sauce)

## FOR THE TOPPING:
230g (8.5oz) dark chocolate, broken into pieces
280ml (scant 1¼ cups) double (or heavy) cream
Flaky sea salt

### FOR THE BASE:

01  Put the biscuits into a food processor and process until finely crushed. Alternatively, put them into a plastic bag and crush with a rolling pin. Tip into a medium mixing bowl, then pour in the melted butter and mix with a spoon until fully combined.

02  Pour it into a deep, loose-bottomed 22cm (8½in) pie tin, pressing down firmly into the base and around the edges with the back of a spoon to create your pie crust.

03  Evenly spread the salted caramel sauce onto the crust.

### FOR THE TOPPING:

04  Put the chocolate and cream in a microwave-safe bowl or jug and microwave on medium heat for 1 minute 20 seconds, then leave to stand for 1 minute. Stir the mix gently until smooth and combined, then pour it over the salted caramel sauce and smooth it out carefully.

05  Sprinkle flaky salt over the top, then chill in the refrigerator for at least 4 hours. Use a hot knife to slice it for a nice clean cut.

06  Store in the refrigerator for up to 3 days.

# VERY BERRY CREAM PIE

## Serves 12

There's nothing like fresh berries and cream for dessert. This pie has a crunchy biscuit base and a thick and luscious vanilla filling topped with cream and mixed berries. Whip it up a few hours before, slice it up and enjoy!

**30 minutes**
**+ 2 hours chilling**

### FOR THE BASE:
300g (10.5oz) digestive biscuits (or graham crackers)
150g (5.25oz) unsalted or salted butter, melted

### FOR THE FILLING:
650ml (2¾ cups) cold double (or heavy) cream
120g (1 cup) icing (powdered) sugar
2 tsp vanilla extract
200g (7oz) full-fat cream cheese, at room temperature

### FOR THE TOPPING:
150g (5.25oz) fresh strawberries, sliced
150g (5.25oz) fresh raspberries
150g (5.25oz) fresh blackberries

### FOR THE BASE:
01  Put the biscuits into a food processor and process until finely crushed. Alternatively, put them into a plastic bag and crush with a rolling pin. Tip into a medium mixing bowl, then pour in the melted butter and mix with a spoon until fully combined.

02  Pour it into a deep, loose-bottomed 22cm (8½in) pie tin, pressing down firmly into the base and around the edges with the back of a spoon to create your pie crust. Pop it in the refrigerator while you make the filling.

### FOR THE FILLING:
03  In a large mixing bowl, whip the cream, icing (powdered) sugar and vanilla extract with an electric hand mixer until soft peaks form, then set aside a quarter in the refrigerator for the topping. Beat the cream cheese into the remaining whipped cream until smooth.

04  Remove the base from the refrigerator and scoop in the cream mixture, smoothing it out to the edges so it's level and smooth on top. Pop it back in the refrigerator for at least 2 hours to set.

### FOR THE TOPPING:
05  Remove the reserved whipped cream from the refrigerator and leave at room temperature for 15–20 minutes, then remove the pie from the refrigerator and dollop the cream on top.

06  Place the berries on top of the cream to decorate and slice with a hot knife for a clean cut. Enjoy!

07  Store in the refrigerator for up to 3 days.

# STRAWBERRY and RASPBERRY ETON MESS

## Serves 6
~~

Eton mess was one of my favourite childhood desserts. I don't even know if you can call this a recipe, to be honest, it's that easy, but I couldn't leave it out. It's the perfect 'throw it together' dessert and it always tastes amazing! The crisp meringue with the fresh fruit and smooth cream are just a dream combination.

### 10 minutes

400g (14oz) fresh strawberries
+ extra to serve (optional)
200g (7oz) fresh raspberries
+ extra to serve (optional)
15g (1 tbsp) granulated sugar
350ml (1½ cups) cold double
(or heavy) cream + extra,
whipped, to serve (optional)
30g (4 tbsp) icing (powdered)
sugar
1 tsp vanilla extract
100g (3.5oz) mascarpone cheese
or full-fat cream cheese,
at room temperature
80g (2.75oz) store-bought
meringues

01  Hull and dice the strawberries and place in a medium mixing bowl with the raspberries, then coat in the granulated sugar.

02  In a large mixing bowl, whip the cream, icing (powdered) sugar and vanilla extract until soft peaks form, then stir in the mascarpone cheese.

03  Break up the meringues, then add them with the fruit to the whipped cream mixture and fold everything together until evenly distributed.

04  Serve in 6 bowls or glasses, topped or layered with extra fruit and whipped cream.

05  Best served straight away. Store covered in the refrigerator for up to 1 day.

Creamy & Frozen Desserts

# WHITE CHOCOLATE SPECULOOS MOUSSE

## Serves 4

This white chocolate and speculoos combo is just perfection. The white chocolate mousse is sweet and creamy, topped with a layer of smooth speculoos spread (cookie butter), sprinkled with caramelised biscuit crumbs. So quick and easy to make, it's a delicious last-minute dessert.

### 5 minutes
#### + 30 minutes chilling

270ml (scant 1¼ cups) cold double (or heavy) cream

150g (5.25oz) white chocolate, melted and cooled slightly

80g (5½ tbsp) speculoos spread/ cookie butter, melted (I use Biscoff)

2 crushed speculoos biscuits, to decorate (optional)

01  In a large mixing bowl, whip the cream to stiff peaks using an electric hand mixer.

02  Pour in the melted white chocolate and beat until combined.

03  Pipe or scoop it into 4 small glasses or jars and smooth the top of each, making sure there's at least a 0.5cm (¼in) gap around the top of each glass.

04  Pour the melted speculoos spread (cookie butter) over the mousse and smooth it out if needed. Sprinkle crushed speculoos biscuit crumbs around the edge of each, if you like.

05  Chill in the refrigerator for at least 30 minutes for best results, or serve straight away.

06  Store in the refrigerator for up to 2 days.

Creamy & Frozen Desserts

# CHOCOLATE TRIFLE

## Serves 12

If you're a fan of chocolate cake and whipped cream, look no further. With layers of chocolate Swiss (cake) roll, chocolate spread, cookies and cream biscuits, brownie chunks and fresh whipped cream, this trifle is a chocolate lover's dream.

### 20 minutes
### + 1 hour chilling

1 litre (4½ cups) cold double (or heavy) cream
200g (1⅔ cups) icing (powdered) sugar
1 tsp vanilla extract
20g (8 tsp) cocoa powder
1 jumbo chocolate Swiss (cake) roll
150g (½ cup) chocolate spread (you could also use chocolate hazelnut spread), melted
20 cookies and cream biscuits (I use Oreos), broken into quarters
Brownie bites, to decorate

01  Put the cream, icing (powdered) sugar and vanilla extract into a large mixing bowl and whip using an electric hand mixer until soft peaks form.

02  Divide the whipped cream in half and transfer one half to another bowl, then fold in the cocoa powder until combined.

03  Slice the Swiss (cake) roll into 1cm (½in) slices, then place a layer into the bottom and around the edges of a 20cm (8in) round x 20cm (8in) deep glass serving dish.

04  Scoop half the chocolate whipped cream over the Swiss roll and smooth it out to the edges, then drizzle one third of the melted chocolate spread over the cream. Scatter one third of the broken biscuits over the chocolate spread, then spread half the vanilla whipped cream over the spread and smooth it out.

05  Repeat with another layer of Swiss roll on top of the cream and around the edges, then layer the remaining chocolate cream, a third of the melted chocolate spread, a third of the broken biscuits and the remaining vanilla whipped cream.

06  To decorate, place the chunks of brownie on top of the cream, evenly scatter over the remaining broken biscuits and drizzle over the remaining melted chocolate spread, or go wild and decorate however you wish.

07  Chill in the refrigerator for at least 1 hour and enjoy!

08  Store in the refrigerator, covered, for up to 3 days.

Creamy & Frozen Desserts

# PEACHES and CREAM TRIFLE

## Serves 12

~~

Tinned peaches were one of my favourite things to eat growing up and this trifle is one of my favourite recipes in this book. The soft vanilla cake, with the cold, creamy custard, the sweet whipped cream and chunks of peaches in fruity apricot jam are just heavenly. It's a great last-minute dessert if you're looking to throw something together, and it's guaranteed to please.

## 30 minutes
### + 1 hour chilling

300g (1 cup) apricot jam
2 x 400g (14oz) can sliced peaches, drained and chopped into chunks
600ml (2½ cups) cold double (or heavy) cream
100g (generous ¾ cup) icing (powdered) sugar
2 tsp vanilla extract
500g (1lb 1oz) store-bought vanilla or madeira (pound) cake, cut into cubes
700g (1lb 5oz) ready-made custard

## TO DECORATE (OPTIONAL)
Fresh peach, sliced
Sprig of mint

01  In a large, heavy-based saucepan, heat the apricot jam over a low heat until melted, then stir in the drained peaches until they're fully coated. Remove from the heat and leave to cool.

02  Put the cream, icing (powdered) sugar and vanilla extract into a large mixing bowl and whip using an electric hand mixer until soft peaks form.

03  Place half the cake cubes into the bottom of a 17cm (7in) round x 15cm (6in) deep glass serving dish.

04  Dollop half the custard evenly on top of the cake, spreading it out to the edges, then dollop half the peach and jam mix over the top, followed by half the whipped cream.

05  Repeat this with the remaining cake, custard, peach and jam mix and whipped cream.

06  Decorate with sliced fresh peaches and a sprig of mint, if you wish.

07  Chill in the refrigerator for at least 1 hour and enjoy!

08  Store in the refrigerator, covered, for up to 3 days.

# SPECULOOS MILKSHAKE

## Serves 2-4

If you love speculoos spread (cookie butter), you have to make this milkshake! It's thick and creamy and packed with speculoos flavours. Dress it up with whipped cream, speculoos spread and biscuits, and enjoy!

## 5 minutes

400g (14oz) good-quality vanilla ice cream, softened

100g (7 tbsp) speculoos spread/ cookie butter (I use Biscoff) + extra, melted, to serve (optional)

4 speculoos biscuits

50ml (¼ cup) whole or semi-skimmed milk

01 Put the ice cream, speculoos spread (cookie butter), biscuits and milk into a blender and blend until smooth and creamy.

02 Drizzle extra melted speculoos spread around the inside of 2 tall glasses, if you like, then pour the milkshake into the glasses.

Creamy & Frozen Desserts

Dress up your milkshakes by topping them with whipped cream and sprinkling over crushed biscuits, as shown in the photo.

# STRAWBERRY CHEESECAKE MILKSHAKE

## Serves 2-4

This milkshake is so thick and creamy. With all the flavours of a strawberry cheesecake in milkshake form, it's a must-try for all cheesecake lovers.

### 5 minutes

300g (10.5oz) good-quality vanilla ice cream, softened
50g (3½ tbsp) full-fat cream cheese, at room temperature
200g (7oz) fresh or frozen strawberries
2 digestive biscuits (or graham crackers)
50ml (¼ cup) whole or semi-skimmed milk
Ready-made strawberry sauce, to serve (optional)

01 Put the ice cream, cream cheese, strawberries, biscuits and milk into a blender and blend until smooth and creamy.

02 Drizzle strawberry sauce around the inside of 2 tall glasses, if you like, then pour the milkshake into the glasses.

Dress up your milkshakes by topping them with whipped cream, sprinkling over crushed biscuits and adding a fresh strawberry on top, as shown in the photo.

# TRAYMAKES

# EASY AND DELICIOUS!

I love how easy and delicious this chapter is.

Many of these recipes only use a few ingredients and they're so much fun to make. If you're new to baking this is a great chapter to get stuck into.

It's packed with rocky roads, biscuit slices and even breakfast bars. You're pretty much just mixing tasty ingredients together, so there's not much that can go wrong (unless you burn the chocolate), but I have confidence in you.

This is a great chapter to experiment with different flavours. For example, if you don't like peanut butter, swap it for speculoos spread (cookie butter) or chocolate spread, it'll still work perfectly and turn out amazing. Have some fun with it and let loose.

## HERE ARE SOME TOP TIPS FOR THIS CHAPTER:

♥ **Melting chocolate:** There's a lot of chocolate melting in this chapter and some chocolates definitely melt better than others. I've found that proper baking chocolate (the type found in the baking aisle) and supermarket own-brand chocolates are best for melting. Expensive, branded versions aren't always the best choice when it comes to melting. Head to page 13 for the best way to melt chocolate.
♥ **Tin size:** I use a standard 20cm (8in) square tin for all my tray bakes, but a 23cm (9in) square tin will also work, your bake will just be slightly thinner. If you want to use a much larger tin, like a 23 x 33cm (9 x 13in) one, double the recipe. If you want to use a much smaller tin, such as a 15cm (6in) round cake tin, halve the recipe. If you want an easy way to check the volume of a tin, fill it with 250ml (1 cup) of water at a time and count the cups until it's full.

So many flavours!

# PEANUT BUTTER CUP ROCKY ROAD

## Serves 16

Here's one for all the peanut butter cup lovers out there. This rocky road has a chocolate peanut butter base and it's packed with peanut butter cups, crunchy biscuits and mini marshmallows. Quick, easy and fun to make and super delicious!

**15 minutes**
+ 1 hour chilling

400g (14oz) milk chocolate
100g (7 tbsp) smooth and creamy peanut butter
250g (9oz) mini peanut butter cups (I use Reese's)
60g (2oz) digestive biscuits (or graham crackers), broken into chunks
70g (1½ cups) mini marshmallows

01  Line a 20cm (8in) baking tin with nonstick baking paper.

02  Melt the chocolate and peanut butter in the microwave on medium heat in 40-second bursts, stirring in between until smooth, then leave to cool slightly so you don't melt the rest of the chocolate when you add it.

03  Put 150g (5.25oz) of the peanut butter cups, the biscuit chunks and mini marshmallows into a large mixing bowl.

04  Pour the chocolate peanut butter mixture into the bowl and stir everything together until fully coated.

05  Scoop it into your prepared tin and smooth it out to the edges. Press the remaining peanut butter cups into the top, then chill in the refrigerator for at least 1 hour. Cut into 16 pieces using a hot knife and enjoy!

06  Store in an airtight container in the refrigerator for up to 4 days.

# CARAMEL SHORTBREAD SLICE

## Serves 16

This slice is chocolatey, crunchy and caramel-y! It's quick and easy to make with just a few ingredients and it tastes so good. Feel free to swap out the chocolate bars for another one of your favourites – it would be delicious with chocolate honeycomb bars.

**15 minutes**
+ 3 hours chilling

350g (12.4oz) digestive biscuits (or graham crackers)
300g (10.5oz) condensed milk
100g (3.5oz) salted butter, melted + 15g (1 tbsp) for the topping
350g (12oz) caramel shortbread chocolate bars (I use Twix), chopped into 0.5cm (¼in) pieces
200g (7oz) milk chocolate, broken into pieces

01  Line a 20cm (8in) square baking tin with nonstick baking paper.

02  Put the biscuits into a food processor and process until finely crushed. Alternatively, put them into a plastic bag and crush with a rolling pin.

03  Tip into a large mixing bowl, then pour in the condensed milk and melted butter and mix with a spoon until fully combined.

04  Fold in 200g (7oz) of the chopped chocolate bars until evenly distributed, then scoop the mix into your prepared tin and smooth it out to the edges.

05  Melt the milk chocolate and 15g (1 tablespoon) of butter in the microwave on medium in 40-second bursts, stirring in between until smooth, then pour it over the base, spread it out and give it a shake for a really smooth finish.

06  Place the remaining chocolate bar pieces over the top to decorate, then chill in the refrigerator for at least 3 hours, or until the base is firm.

07  Use a hot knife to cut it into 16 pieces and enjoy!

08  Store in an airtight container in the refrigerator for up to 4 days.

Traymakes

# CARAMEL PEANUT SLICE

## Serves 16

If you love peanuts and caramel together, this slice is for you. It's packed with caramel peanut chocolate bars and topped with a layer of chocolate with a peanut butter swirl. Easy to make and so delicious.

### 15 minutes
#### + 3 hours chilling

350g (12.4oz) digestive biscuits (or graham crackers)
100g (3.5oz) salted butter, melted + 15g (1 tbsp) for the topping
300g (10.5oz) ready-made caramel (I use Carnation)
250g (9oz) caramel peanut chocolate bars (I use Snickers), chopped into 0.5cm (¼in) pieces
200g (7oz) milk chocolate, broken into pieces
25g (2½ tbsp) smooth and creamy peanut butter, melted

01  Line a 20cm (8in) square baking tin with nonstick baking paper.

02  Put the biscuits into a food processor and process until finely crushed. Alternatively, put them into a plastic bag and crush with a rolling pin.

03  Tip into a large mixing bowl, then pour in the melted butter and caramel and mix with a spoon until fully combined.

04  Fold in the chopped peanut caramel chocolate bars until evenly distributed, then scoop the mix into your prepared tin and smooth it out to the edges.

05  Melt the milk chocolate and 15g (1 tablespoon) of butter in the microwave on medium in 40-second bursts, stirring in between until smooth, then pour it over the base, spread it out and give it a shake for a really smooth finish.

06  Drizzle over the melted peanut butter and swirl it through with a skewer or knife to make a pretty pattern, then chill in the refrigerator for at least 3 hours, or until the base is firm.

07  Use a hot knife to cut it into 16 pieces and enjoy!

08  Store in an airtight container in the refrigerator for up to 4 days.

# LEMON SLICE

## Serves 16
~~

This lemon slice is just heavenly! The frosting is sweet, tangy and refreshing and goes perfectly with the buttery lemon shortbread base. It's delicious at any time of the year and it's super easy to make.

**15 minutes**
+ 2 hours chilling

### FOR THE BASE:
320g (11oz) shortbread biscuits
100g (3.5oz) unsalted butter, melted
150g (5.25oz) condensed milk
Zest of 1 lemon

### FOR THE FROSTING:
200g (1⅔ cups) icing (powdered) sugar
20g (½ tbsp) unsalted butter, softened
60ml (4 tbsp) lemon juice (about 1–1½ lemons)
Zest of 1 lemon, to decorate

### FOR THE BASE:

01  Line a 20cm (8in) square baking tin with nonstick baking paper.

02  Put the biscuits into a food processor and process until finely crushed. Alternatively, put them into a plastic bag and crush with a rolling pin.

03  Tip into a large mixing bowl, then pour in the melted butter, condensed milk and lemon zest and mix with a spoon until fully combined.

04  Scoop the mix into your prepared tin and smooth it out to the edges.

### FOR THE FROSTING:

05  Add half the icing (powdered) sugar, the butter and lemon juice to a medium mixing bowl and beat with an electric hand mixer until combined, then add the remaining icing sugar and beat until smooth and creamy. Add more lemon juice if needed to make it easier to spread.

06  Spread it over the base and decorate with lemon zest, then chill in the refrigerator for 2 hours, or until the base is firm. Cut into 16 pieces and enjoy!

07  Store in an airtight container in the refrigerator for up to 4 days.

# SPECULOOS TIFFIN

### Serves 16

This tiffin is so chocolatey, packed with crunchy caramelised biscuits, with a milk chocolate topping and speculoos spread (cookie butter) swirl. It's quick and easy to do and definitely a must-make for speculoos lovers!

## 15 minutes
### + 2 hours 30 minutes chilling

### FOR THE BASE:
400g (14oz) speculoos biscuits
  (I use Biscoff)
200g (7oz) salted butter
70g (5 tbsp) speculoos spread/
  cookie butter (I use Biscoff)
30ml (2 tbsp) golden syrup
  or honey
30g (4 tbsp) cocoa powder
50g (¼ cup) granulated sugar

### FOR THE TOPPING:
250g (9oz) milk chocolate, broken
  into pieces
15g (1 tbsp) salted butter
50g (3½ tbsp) speculoos spread/
  cookie butter, melted

### FOR THE BASE:

01  Line a 20cm (8in) square baking tin with nonstick baking paper.

02  Put three quarters of the biscuits into a food processor and process until finely crushed. Alternatively, put them into a plastic bag and crush with a rolling pin. Break or chop the remaining biscuits into small chunks.

03  In a large saucepan, melt the butter, speculoos spread (cookie butter), golden syrup or honey, cocoa powder and sugar over a low heat, stirring constantly, until smooth and combined.

04  Remove from the heat, then pour in all the biscuits and coat in the mixture.

05  Scoop it into your prepared tin and press it down really firmly with the back of a spoon, then chill in the refrigerator for 30 minutes.

### FOR THE TOPPING:

06  When the base has been in the refrigerator for 30 minutes, melt the milk chocolate and 15g (1 tablespoon) of butter in the microwave on medium in 40-second bursts, stirring in between until smooth, then pour it over the base, spread it out and give the tin a shake for a really smooth finish.

07  Drizzle over the melted speculoos spread and swirl it through with a skewer or knife to make a pretty pattern, then chill in the refrigerator for at least 2 hours, or until the base is firm.

08  To serve, remove from the refrigerator and leave to stand for about 10 minutes, then cut into 16 squares and enjoy!

09  Store in an airtight container in the refrigerator or at room temperature for up to 4 days.

# MILK and WHITE CHOCOLATE ROCKY ROAD

## Serves 16

~~

If you love white chocolate, mini marshmallows and hazelnut flavours, you will love this rocky road. It's super easy to make with just a few ingredients and it will definitely satisfy a sweet tooth.

**15 minutes**
*+ 1 hour chilling*

500g (1lb) white chocolate, broken into pieces

50g (3½ tbsp) unsalted butter

150g (5.25oz) mini milk and white chocolate bars (I use Kinder), broken into pieces

160g (5.5oz) chocolate hazelnut wafers (I use Kinder Bueno), broken into pieces

50g (1 cup) mini pink and white marshmallows

01  Line a 20cm (8in) baking tin with nonstick baking paper.

02  Melt the white chocolate and butter in the microwave on medium in 40-second bursts, stirring in between until smooth, then leave to cool slightly so you don't melt the rest of the chocolate when you add it.

03  Put the milk and white chocolate bars, half the chocolate hazelnut wafers and the mini marshmallows into a large mixing bowl.

04  Pour the white chocolate mixture into the bowl and stir everything together until fully coated.

05  Scoop it into your prepared tin and smooth it out to the edges. Press the remaining chocolate hazelnut wafers into the top, then chill in the refrigerator for at least 1 hour. Cut into 16 pieces using a hot knife and enjoy!

06  Store in an airtight container in the refrigerator for up to 4 days.

Traymakes

# CHOCOLATE HAZELNUT TRUFFLE ROCKY ROAD

## Serves 16

Oooh this rocky road is indulgent. It's nutty and chocolatey and so deliciously rich. Packed with chocolate hazelnut truffles, chocolate hazelnut spread, mini marshmallows and biscuit chunks, it's a chocolate lover's dream!

**15 minutes**
+ 1 hour chilling

400g (14oz) milk chocolate
100g (5½ tbsp) chocolate hazelnut spread (I use Nutella)
200g (7oz) chocolate hazelnut truffles (I use Ferrero Rocher)
60g (2oz) digestive biscuits (or graham crackers), broken into chunks
70g (1½ cups) white mini marshmallows

01  Line a 20cm (8in) baking tin with nonstick baking paper.

02  Melt the chocolate and chocolate hazelnut spread in the microwave on medium heat in 40-second bursts, stirring in between until smooth, then leave to cool slightly so you don't melt the rest of the chocolate when you add it.

03  Put the chocolate hazelnut truffles, biscuit chunks and mini marshmallows into a large mixing bowl.

04  Pour the chocolate mixture into the bowl and stir everything together until fully coated.

05  Scoop the mix into your prepared tin and smooth it out to the edges, then chill in the refrigerator for at least 1 hour. Cut into 16 pieces using a hot knife and enjoy!

06  Store in an airtight container in the refrigerator for up to 4 days.

# APRICOT BREAKFAST BARS

## Makes 10

These oat bars are sweet and chewy, packed with honey and juicy dried apricots. They're easy to make and absolutely delicious. Perfect for when you need a quick snack and a burst of energy.

### 15 minutes
### + 5 hours chilling

85g (5½ tbsp) salted butter
35g (3 tbsp) brown sugar
120ml (½ cup) honey
130g (1⅓ cups) rolled oats
25g (1 cup) puffed rice cereal
1 tsp ground cinnamon
130g (4.75oz) dried apricots,
   chopped into small chunks

01  Line a 20cm (8in) baking tin with nonstick baking paper.

02  In a medium saucepan, melt the butter, sugar and honey over a low heat and cook until the mixture thickens (at least 10 minutes).

03  Put the oats, cereal, cinnamon and chopped apricots into a large mixing bowl, then pour the honey mixture into the bowl and stir until everything is fully coated.

04  Scoop it into your prepared tin and press down firmly with the back of a spoon. The mix will be sticky!

05  Chill in the refrigerator for at least 5 hours, then cut into 10 bars and enjoy!

06  Store in an airtight container in the refrigerator for up to 5 days.

141

Traymakes

# IN THE MICROWAVE

# GENIUS, IF YOU ASK ME

The microwave was my saviour when I was younger.  Whenever my mum wouldn't let me turn on the oven to cook something, the microwave was always there for me.

I love the convenience of baking in the microwave and I love that everything stays so moist (if you cook it properly, that is). I always enjoyed those little microwave sticky toffee puddings and the syrup sponge ones tasted amazing too. Genius, if you ask me.

Mug cakes are always a big hit and they're so quick and easy to make, but there are more than mug cakes in this chapter. I'm talking microwave brownies (page 150), a microwave cookie (page 146) and a whole microwave chocolate cake (page 148), good enough for a birthday, that no one would know you hadn't baked in the oven.

If you've never tried baking in the microwave, this is your chance.

## HERE ARE SOME TOP TIPS TO HELP YOU WITH THIS CHAPTER:

♥ **All cooking times are a guide:** Let me start by saying that all microwaves are different (the one I have right now doesn't even rotate! I have to turn it myself to make sure it cooks evenly). Please watch your bake to ensure it doesn't overcook. You're better off cooking on medium (around 500W) than high. Ovens have temperatures for a reason, treat the microwave in the same way.
♥ **Materials:** Be sure to always use microwave-safe materials. The material, shape and size of what you're cooking in (for instance, the mug) will make a difference to how your recipe cooks. Just another reason to pay close attention to your bake and the 'doneness' cues.
♥ **Heat-treat your flour:** See page 13.
♥ **Eggs:**  Recipes that include eggs should reach at least 74°C (165°F) to make sure they're cooked properly.

Super speedy!

FAN FAVOURITE · FAN FAVOURITE ·

# MICROWAVE CHOCOLATE CHIP COOKIE

### Makes 1

This cookie is so quick and easy to make in just 5 minutes. It's warm and gooey, sweet and delicious and it's packed with chocolate chips. Perfect for when you want a cookie, but don't want to make a whole batch.

### 5 minutes

15g (1 tbsp) salted butter, melted
15g (1 tbsp) granulated sugar
15g (1 tbsp) light brown sugar
1 large egg yolk
½ tsp vanilla extract
20g (generous 2 tbsp) plain (all-purpose) flour, heat-treated (see page 13)
1 tbsp chocolate chips + some for the top (optional)

01  Put the melted butter, granulated sugar and light brown sugar into a microwave-safe ramekin about 8cm (3¼in) deep x 5.5cm (2¼in) high, and stir with a spoon until fully combined.

02  Add the egg yolk and vanilla extract and mix until combined.

03  Add the heat-treated flour and fold in until just a few streaks of flour remain, then add the chocolate chips and fold in until evenly distributed.

04  Level out the top, then press in a few more chocolate chips if you wish.

05  Microwave on medium for 45–50 seconds, or until the top looks moist, but no wet batter remains. Make sure you don't overcook it, otherwise your cookie will become dry.

06  Let to stand for 1 minute, then serve warm.

You could also split the mix into 2 smaller ramekins. If doing this, microwave separately for 20–30 seconds.

FAN FAVOURITE · FAN FAVOURITE ·

# MICROWAVE CHOCOLATE CAKE

### Serves 8

No one will ever know this cake was made in the microwave! It's unbelievably soft and moist, topped with a rich chocolate ganache. If you want to make a cake, but don't want to turn on the oven, this chocolate cake is perfect. Plus it's so easy to make and you don't even need any eggs.

## 20 minutes
### + cooling

### FOR THE CAKE:
150g (1¼ cups) plain (all-purpose) flour, heat-treated (see page 13)
100g (½ cup) granulated sugar
60g (8 tbsp) cocoa powder
2 tsp baking powder
90g (6 tbsp) unsalted butter, melted, or 6 tbsp vegetable oil
380ml (scant 1⅔ cups) warm water

### FOR THE TOPPING:
150g (5.25oz) dark chocolate, broken into pieces
150ml (⅔ cup) double (or heavy) cream

### FOR THE CAKE:

01  Grease and line an 18cm (7in) round microwave-safe cake mould with nonstick baking paper.

02  In a large mixing bowl, mix together the flour, granulated sugar, cocoa powder and baking powder using a balloon whisk until combined.

03  Pour in the melted butter or vegetable oil and warm water and beat until runny and smooth.

04  Pour the batter into your cake mould.

05  Microwave on medium heat for 5–6 minutes until a toothpick inserted into the centre of the cake comes out with a few moist crumbs on it. Check the cake about 1 minute before you think it's cooked. If you overcook it, it can become dry and rubbery.

06  Leave to cool slightly, then flip it upside down onto a wire rack and remove the baking paper, then leave to cool completely.

### FOR THE TOPPING:

07  Put the chocolate and cream into a microwave-safe jug or small mixing bowl and microwave on medium for 1 minute 20 seconds. Leave to stand for 1 minute, then stir gently until smooth and combined.

08  Transfer to a serving plate and pour the ganache over the cooled cake, letting it drip over the edges slightly, and smooth it out.

09  Let the ganache set at room temperature, then cut into 8 slices and serve. Enjoy!

10  Store in an airtight container in the refrigerator for up to 4 days. If eating the cake after it's been in the refrigerator, leave at room temperature for at least 30 minutes before serving.

# MICROWAVE BROWNIES

## Makes 8

These brownies are so soft and chocolatey and they're packed with chocolate chips. They're the perfect alternative when you want a quick and easy brownie without turning on the oven.

### 7 minutes

45g (1.75oz) dark chocolate (50% cocoa), broken into pieces

30g (2 tbsp) salted butter

45g (3 tbsp) caster (superfine) or granulated sugar

30ml (2 tbsp) warm milk

70g (½ cup) plain (all-purpose) flour, heat-treated (see page 13)

50g (3½ tbsp) milk or dark chocolate chips + a handful for the top

01 Grease and line a 10 x 18cm (4 x 7in) microwave-safe dish (or a dish of similar volume) with nonstick baking paper.

02 Put the dark chocolate and butter into a small microwave-safe bowl and microwave on medium in 40-second bursts, stirring in between until smooth.

03 Add the sugar and warm milk and stir in with a spoon until combined, then fold in the flour, followed by the chocolate chips.

04 Scoop the batter into your prepared dish and smooth it out, then sprinkle a handful of chocolate chips on top.

05 Microwave on medium for 2 minutes, or until there's no wet batter left (check it at 1 minute 30 seconds as it may be ready). Make sure you don't overcook the batter as it can become dry and rubbery.

06 Leave to cool, then remove from the dish and cut into 8 pieces. Enjoy!

07 Store in an airtight container at room temperature for up to 5 days.

# MICROWAVE VANILLA CAKE

## Serves 8

Vanilla cake with vanilla buttercream and sprinkles is my kind of cake! This cake is soft, moist, sweet and absolutely delicious. No one will know it was made in the microwave.

**20 minutes**
+ cooling

### FOR THE CAKE:

65g salted butter, softened
75g (6 tbsp) caster (superfine) or granulated sugar
55g (3 tbsp) Greek or plain yogurt, at room temperature
1 tsp vanilla extract
130g (1 cup) plain (all-purpose) flour, heat-treated (see page 13)
1 ½ tsp baking powder
150ml (⅔ cup) milk, at room temperature

### FOR THE BUTTERCREAM:

80g (5½ tbsp) unsalted butter, softened
100g (generous ¾ cup) icing (powdered) sugar
1 tsp vanilla extract
Sprinkles, to decorate (optional)

### FOR THE CAKE:

01  Grease and line an 18cm (7in) round microwave-safe cake mould with nonstick baking paper.

02  In a large mixing bowl, cream together the butter and sugar with a spoon until smooth, then add the yogurt and vanilla extract and mix with a balloon whisk until combined (don't worry if it looks a little lumpy at this stage).

03  Add the flour, baking powder and milk and mix in. The batter should be thick and smooth. Pour the batter into your prepared cake mould and level it out.

04  Microwave on medium for 5–6 minutes, or until a toothpick inserted into the centre of the cake comes out with a few moist crumbs on it. Check the cake about 1 minute before you think it's cooked. If you overcook it, it can become dry and rubbery.

05  Leave to cool slightly, then flip it upside down onto a wire rack and remove the baking paper, then leave to cool completely.

### FOR THE BUTTERCREAM:

06  Beat the butter with an electric hand mixer until creamy, then beat in half the icing (powdered) sugar. Once combined, beat in the rest of the icing sugar and the vanilla extract until smooth and creamy. The buttercream should be thick, but spreadable.

07  Spread it over the cooled cake, then decorate with sprinkles or however you wish. Cut into 8 slices and serve. Enjoy!

08  Store in an airtight container at room temperature for up to 4 days.

# LEMON DRIZZLE MUG CAKE

## Serves 1-2

This mug cake is soft, sweet and zesty. It's super lemony and topped with a crunchy lemon drizzle (that's the best bit, if you ask me).

## 7 minutes

### FOR THE CAKE:
45g (4½ tbsp) plain (all-purpose) flour, heat-treated (see page 13)
45g (3 tbsp) granulated sugar
½ tsp baking powder
30ml (2 tbsp) milk
30ml (2 tbsp) lemon juice
30ml (2 tbsp) vegetable oil

### FOR THE DRIZZLE:
2 tsp lemon juice
15g (1 tbsp) granulated sugar

### FOR THE CAKE:

01 Add the flour, sugar and baking powder to a large microwave-safe mug, or split between 2 smaller mugs if making 2, and mix them together.

02 Add the milk, lemon juice and vegetable oil and mix until smooth.

03 Microwave on medium for 1 minute 30 seconds, or until a toothpick inserted into the middle of the cake comes out with a few moist crumbs on it. Check your mug cake at the 1 minute mark to make sure it doesn't overflow.

### FOR THE DRIZZLE:

04 While the cake is cooking, mix together the lemon juice and sugar in a small bowl or ramekin.

05 Once the cake is cooked, pour over the drizzle, then leave to cool for 1 minute before eating. Enjoy!

FAN FAVOURITE · FAN FAVOURITE

# CINNAMON SWIRL MUG CAKE

## Serves 1-2

This mug cake is super soft and moist, packed with swirls of sweet cinnamon.
If you love cinnamon and warm cake, you have to make this one.

### 7 minutes

**FOR THE CAKE:**
60g (6 tbsp) plain (all-purpose)
  flour, heat-treated (see
  page 13)
45g (3 tbsp) granulated sugar
½ tsp baking powder
60ml (4 tbsp) water
40ml (3 tbsp) oil or melted butter
½ tsp vanilla extract

**FOR THE CINNAMON SWIRL:**
½ tbsp melted butter
1 tbsp light brown sugar
¼ tsp ground cinnamon

**FOR THE CINNAMON SUGAR:**
1 tsp granulated sugar
⅛ tsp ground cinnamon

01   Put all the ingredients for the cake into a small mixing bowl and
      beat together until smooth.

02   In a small ramekin or bowl, mix together the ingredients for the
      cinnamon swirl until combined.

03   Pour half the cake batter into a large microwave-safe mug or
      split between 2 smaller mugs if making 2.

04   Dollop or pipe half the cinnamon swirl mix on top of the batter.

05   Pour the remaining batter on top and smooth it out, then pipe
      the remaining cinnamon swirl on top in a spiral pattern.

06   Mix together the sugar and cinnamon to make the cinnamon
      sugar, then sprinkle this on top.

07   Microwave on medium for 1 minute 20 seconds, or until there's
      no wet batter remaining. Check your mug cake at the 1 minute
      mark to make sure it doesn't overflow.

08   Leave to rest for 1 minute, as it will be very hot, then dig in
      and enjoy!

FAN FAVOURITE · FAN FAVOURITE

# SPRINKLE DOUGHNUT MUG CAKE

## Serves 1-2

I called this a doughnut mug cake because it reminds me of the big pink sprinkle doughnut from *The Simpsons*. The cake is soft, moist and vanilla-y, topped with a simple sweet glaze and, of course, lots of sprinkles. It's quick and easy to make and absolutely delicious.

### 7 minutes

**FOR THE CAKE:**

40g (4 tbsp) plain (all-purpose) flour, heat-treated (see page 13)
30g (2 tbsp) granulated sugar
¼ tsp baking powder
40ml (3 tbsp) warm water
25ml (1½ tbsp) oil or melted butter
½ tsp vanilla extract

**FOR THE GLAZE:**

15g (2 tbsp) icing (powdered) sugar
1 tsp milk
Pink food colouring (optional)
Sprinkles, to decorate

**FOR THE CAKE:**

01 Put all the ingredients for the cake into a small mixing bowl and beat together until smooth.

02 Pour the cake batter into a large microwave-safe mug or split between 2 smaller mugs if making 2.

03 Microwave on medium for 1 minute 20 seconds, or until there's no wet batter remaining. Check your mug cake at the 1 minute mark to make sure it doesn't overflow.

**FOR THE GLAZE:**

04 While the cake is in the microwave, mix together the icing (powdered) sugar and milk until smooth. Add more icing sugar or more milk to reach the consistency you want. You can also add a very small amount of food colouring here if you want to colour the glaze.

05 Pour the glaze over the warm cake, smoothing it out to the edges, then decorate with sprinkles.

06 Leave to rest for 1 minute, as it will be very hot, then dig in and enjoy!

# RED VELVET MUG CAKE

## Serves 1-2

Soft and warm cake with a subtle chocolatey-vanilla taste, topped with cream cheese frosting and a dusting of icing (powdered) sugar. If you love red velvet cake, you need to try this easy mug cake version.

## 7 minutes

### FOR THE CAKE:

45ml (3 tbsp) milk

½ tsp lemon juice or white vinegar

30g (3½ tbsp) plain (all-purpose) flour, heat-treated (see page 13)

25g (1½ tbsp) granulated or caster (superfine) sugar

½ tsp cocoa powder

⅛ tsp baking powder

22ml (1½ tbsp) vegetable oil

Red food colouring

20g (1½ tbsp) white chocolate chips (optional)

### FOR THE CREAM CHEESE FROSTING:

40g (3 tbsp) full-fat cream cheese, at room temperature

15g (2 tbsp) icing (powdered) sugar + extra for dusting

### FOR THE CAKE:

01 Put the milk and lemon juice into a small mixing bowl and mix them together with a fork, then add the flour, sugar, cocoa powder, baking powder, vegetable oil and red food colouring and beat everything together until smooth. Fold in the white chocolate chips, if using.

02 Pour the cake batter into a large microwave-safe mug or split between 2 smaller mugs if making 2.

03 Microwave on medium for 1 minute 20 seconds, or until there's no wet batter remaining. Check your mug cake at the 1 minute mark to make sure it doesn't overflow.

### FOR THE CREAM CHEESE FROSTING:

04 While the cake is in the microwave, mix together the cream cheese and icing (powdered) sugar until smooth. Add more icing sugar if you want to thicken it up.

05 Leave to rest for 1 minute, then dollop the cream cheese frosting onto the middle of your cake and dust with icing sugar. Enjoy!

# ON THE STOVE

# SO MANY THINGS TO MAKE!

There are so many things you can make on the stove. I love this chapter because it's so versatile. It has everything from French toast rolls and pancakes, to rice crispy bars and millionaire's shortbread.

You'll find some of my most popular recipes from social media in this chapter, such as my Chocolate-stuffed French Toast Sticks (page 176) and Cinnamon Roll Pancakes (page 182), plus newbies like the White Chocolate Millionaire's Shortbread (page 173). Yum!

A lot of these recipes are quick and easy to make and ready to eat almost straight away; that's the beauty of using the stove.

There's something for everyone here, whether you're looking for a fun breakfast or brunch, or a crowd-pleasing dessert to bring to a party.

## HERE ARE SOME TOP TIPS TO HELP YOU WITH THIS CHAPTER:

♥ **Caramel:** Caramel can be intimidating if you've never made it before, but it's actually really easy. The more you make it, the easier it'll become. Caramel should reach 120°C (275°F) but if you don't have a thermometer, you can check to see whether your caramel is done by using the 'soft ball stage' test: drop 1 teaspoon of the caramel into a glass of very cold water. If it forms a soft ball, the caramel is ready. Easy as that.

♥ **Heat:** When you're cooking in a saucepan or frying pan, pay attention to the heat of your pan. When cooking pancakes and French toast, you're better having the heat too low than too high, as no one wants a burnt breakfast.

Crowd-pleaser!

# CINNAMON S'MORES MARSHMALLOW BARS

## Makes 16

Cinnamon cereal is top tier, if you ask me, and it works so perfectly in this recipe! The marshmallows are all gooey and they're packed with chocolate chips. It has all the flavours of s'mores in a bar, you'll be wanting s'more... (sorry).

**15 minutes**
+ 1-2 hours cooling

75g (5 tbsp) salted butter
280g (3½ cups) + 75g (1½ cups) white mini marshmallows
250g (9oz) cinnamon crunch cereal (I use Curiously Cinnamon in the UK and Cinnamon Toast Crunch in the US)
50g (3½ tbsp) milk chocolate chips or chunks

01 Line a 20cm (8in) square baking tin with nonstick baking paper.

02 In a large saucepan, melt the butter and 280g (3½ cups) of the marshmallows over a low–medium heat, stirring regularly, until fully combined.

03 Turn off the heat and fold in the cereal until fully coated, then fold in the remaining marshmallows.

04 Scoop the mix into your prepared baking tin and spread it out to the edges, pressing down gently, then sprinkle the chocolate chips or chunks on top.

05 Leave to cool at room temperature for 1–2 hours, then cut into 16 squares and enjoy!

06 Store in an airtight container at room temperature for up to 4 days.

# MILK and WHITE CHOCOLATE CRISPY BARS

## Makes 9-16

These marshmallow crispy bars are sweet and gooey, with a satisfying crunch, topped with smooth and creamy milk and white chocolate. Quick and easy to make with just 5 ingredients, they're perfect for parties and always a crowd-pleaser.

### 15 minutes
### + 1 hour chilling

125g (5 cups) puffed rice cereal
60g (4 tbsp) salted butter
300g (6 cups) mini marshmallows
24 mini milk and white chocolate bars, 8 (100g/3.5oz) for the base, 16 (200g/7oz) for the topping
4½ mini milk and white chocolate bars, halved, to decorate (optional)

01  Line a 20cm (8in) square baking tin with nonstick baking paper.

02  Put the puffed rice cereal into a large mixing bowl and set aside for now.

03  Put the butter, mini marshmallows and 100g (3.5oz) of the chocolate into a large saucepan, then stir continuously over a low–medium heat until melted and smooth.

04  Pour the mixture over the puffed rice cereal and stir gently until fully coated.

05  Scoop the mix into your prepared tin and press it down with the base of a wet glass or the back of a wet spoon so it doesn't stick.

06  Melt 200g (7oz) of the chocolate in a double boiler (see pages 13–14). Alternatively, put it into a small microwave-safe bowl and melt in the microwave on medium in 1-minute bursts, stirring until smooth. Pour the melted chocolate over the base and level it out, then give the tin a shake for a smooth finish.

07  Place the halved chocolate bars on top as shown in the photo, if using.

08  Chill in the refrigerator for 1 hour, or until the topping has set. Cut into 9–16 squares and enjoy!

09  Store in an airtight container at room temperature for up to 5 days.

# CHOCOLATE CORNFLAKE SLICE

## *Makes 16*

This recipe feels so nostalgic to me. There's just something about chocolate and cornflakes together that tastes so good and the texture is so moreish. Super easy to make with just a few ingredients and definitely a crowd-pleaser.

**15 minutes**
+ 1 hour 30 minutes cooling
+ chilling

### FOR THE BASE:
300g (10.5oz) milk chocolate
40g (3 tbsp) salted butter
30ml (2 tbsp) honey or
  golden syrup
110g (4 cups) cornflakes

### FOR THE TOPPING:
200g (7oz) milk chocolate
15g (1 tbsp) salted butter

### FOR THE CAKE:

01  Line a 20cm (8in) square baking tin with nonstick baking paper.

02  Put the chocolate, butter and honey or golden syrup into a large saucepan and melt over a low–medium heat, stirring constantly, until smooth.

03  Turn off the heat, and fold in the cornflakes until fully coated.

04  Scoop the mix into your prepared baking tin and spread it out to the edges, pressing down gently.

### FOR THE TOPPING:

05  Melt the chocolate and butter in a double boiler (see pages 13–14). Alternatively, put them into a small microwave-safe bowl and microwave in 40-second bursts, stirring in between until melted and smooth.

06  Pour the melted chocolate over the base and smooth it out to the edges. Give the tin a shake for a flawless finish, then chill in the refrigerator for 30 minutes, or until the topping has set.

07  Cut into 16 pieces using a hot knife and enjoy!

08  Store in an airtight container at room temperature for up to 4 days.

# WHITE CHOCOLATE MILLIONAIRE'S SHORTBREAD

ONE TIN · ONE TIN · ONE TIN · ONE TIN ·

## Makes 16

Thick, sweet and creamy, with a buttery shortbread base, a gooey caramel filling and a smooth white chocolate topping. If you love white chocolate, this is the one for you.

**30 minutes**
*+ 2 hours cooling + chilling*

### FOR THE BASE:
450g (15oz) shortbread biscuits
120g (8½ tbsp) salted butter, melted

### FOR THE CARAMEL:
1 x 397g (14oz) can condensed milk
90g (6 tbsp) salted butter
100g (½ cup) light brown sugar
15ml (1 tbsp) golden syrup

### FOR THE TOPPING:
200g (7oz) white chocolate, broken into pieces + 16 squares to decorate (optional)
100ml (scant ½ cup) double (or heavy) cream

### FOR THE BASE:

01 Line a 20cm (8in) square baking tin with nonstick baking paper.

02 Put the biscuits into a food processor and process until finely crushed. Alternatively, put them into a plastic bag and crush with a rolling pin. Tip into a medium mixing bowl, then add the melted butter and mix with a spoon until fully combined. Press it into the bottom of your tin with the back of a spoon. Set aside.

### FOR THE CARAMEL:

03 Put the condensed milk, butter, sugar and golden syrup into a large saucepan. Stir constantly over a low–medium heat until the sugar has dissolved and everything has fully combined. Turn up the heat to medium–high and continue to stir until the mixture thickens and starts to bubble continuously.

04 Test if it is ready by using the 'soft ball stage' test – drop 1 teaspoon of the caramel into a glass of very cold water. If it forms a soft ball, it's ready. Pour it over the base and carefully smooth it out with the back of a spoon if needed. Leave to set at room temperature for at least 1 hour until completely cooled.

### FOR THE TOPPING:

05 Once the caramel has cooled, put the white chocolate and cream into a microwave-safe bowl and microwave on high for 1 minute 20 seconds (the cream should be warm enough to melt the chocolate without boiling and curdling). Leave to stand for 2 minutes, then stir until the cream and chocolate start to come together. Continue to stir until smooth and creamy. Pour it over the caramel, smoothing it out gently with the back of a metal spoon or spatula, then place the additional pieces of white chocolate on top as shown in the photo, if using.

06 Chill in the refrigerator for 1 hour until the topping has completely set. Cut into 16 squares and enjoy!

07 Store in an airtight container in the refrigerator for up to 5 days.

# SPECULOOS MILLIONAIRE'S BARS

## *Makes 16*

A thick, buttery speculoos biscuit base, a layer of gooey homemade caramel, topped with speculoos white chocolate and a speculoos swirl. This recipe doesn't skimp on speculoos!

## 30 minutes
### + 2 hours cooling + chilling

### FOR THE BASE:
500g (1lb) speculoos biscuits (I use Biscoff)
200g (7oz) salted butter, melted

### FOR THE CARAMEL:
1 x 397g (14oz) can condensed milk
90g (6 tbsp) unsalted butter
100g (½ cup) light brown sugar
1 tsp salt
15ml (1 tbsp) golden syrup

### FOR THE TOPPING:
250g (9oz) white chocolate, broken into pieces
100g (7 tbsp) speculoos spread/cookie butter (I use Biscoff) + 50g (3½ tbsp), melted, for the swirl

### FOR THE BASE:

01 Line a 20cm (8in) square baking tin with nonstick baking paper.

02 Put the biscuits into a food processor and process until finely crushed. Alternatively, put them into a plastic bag and crush with a rolling pin. Tip into a medium mixing bowl, then pour in the melted butter and mix with a spoon until fully combined.

03 Press the mixture firmly into the bottom of your prepared tin with the back of a spoon. Set aside.

### FOR THE CARAMEL:

04 Put the condensed milk, butter, sugar, salt and golden syrup into a large saucepan. Stir constantly over a low–medium heat until the sugar has dissolved and everything has melted and fully combined.

05 Turn up the heat to medium–high and continue to stir until the mixture thickens and starts to bubble continuously.

06 Test if it is ready by using the 'soft ball stage' test – drop 1 teaspoon of caramel into a glass of very cold water. If it forms a soft ball, it's ready. Pour the caramel over the base and smooth it out with the back of a spoon if needed. Leave to set at room temperature for at least 1 hour until completely cooled.

### FOR THE TOPPING:

07 Once the caramel has cooled, put the white chocolate and speculoos spread (cookie butter) into a microwave-safe bowl and microwave on medium in 40-second bursts, stirring in between until melted and smooth.

08 Pour the topping over the caramel, smoothing it gently with the back of a metal spoon, then drizzle over the remaining speculoos spread and swirl it with a skewer to make a pattern.

09 Chill in the refrigerator for 1 hour until the topping has completely set. Cut into 16 squares and enjoy!

10 Store in an airtight container in the refrigerator or at room temperature for up to 5 days.

FAN FAVOURITE · FAN FAVOURITE ·

# CHOCOLATE-STUFFED FRENCH TOAST STICKS

## Makes 9

This is one of my most popular recipes ever on social media. Soft, warm, doughy bread stuffed with chocolate hazelnut spread, coated in cinnamon sugar. These toast sticks are so simple, but oh so delicious!

### 15 minutes

6 slices of soft bread
60–100g (3–5 tbsp) chocolate hazelnut spread (I use Nutella)
2 large eggs
60ml (4 tbsp) milk
1 tsp vanilla extract
Knob of butter, for frying
45g (3 tbsp) granulated sugar
1 tsp ground cinnamon

01  Cut the crusts off the slices of bread (or you can leave them on if you like).

02  Spread the chocolate hazelnut spread over 3 slices of the bread, all the way to the edges, then place another slice of bread on top of each to make a sandwich.

03  Slice each sandwich into 3 batons using a bread knife and a sawing motion so you don't crush them.

04  In a medium mixing bowl, beat together the eggs, milk and vanilla extract until combined, then dip the batons in the mix so they're fully covered; you don't need to soak them.

05  Melt a knob of butter in a large frying pan and toast the sticks over a low heat until golden brown on each side.

06  While they're cooking, mix together the sugar and cinnamon in a bowl, then coat the sticks in the mix while they're still hot. Serve straight away with whatever you wish, enjoy!

Swap the chocolate hazelnut spread for speculoos spread (cookie butter), if you prefer.

FAN FAVOURITE · FAN FAVOURITE ·

# CINNAMON ROLL FRENCH TOAST

## Makes 8

Two of my favourite things combined: French toast and cinnamon rolls! These French toast rolls are stuffed with cinnamon butter, coated in cinnamon sugar and drizzled with cream cheese frosting. They're warm, sweet and cinnamony and they taste so good! One of my most popular recipes on social media.

## 20 minutes

### FOR THE CINNAMON BUTTER:
70g (5 tbsp) unsalted butter, softened
50g (¼ cup) light brown sugar
1 tbsp ground cinnamon

### FOR THE FRENCH TOAST:
8 slices of soft bread
2 large eggs
60ml (4 tbsp) milk
1 tsp vanilla extract
Knob of butter, for frying

### FOR THE CREAM CHEESE FROSTING:
20g (1½ tbsp) unsalted butter, softened
60g (4 tbsp) full-fat cream cheese, at room temperature
25g (3½ tbsp) icing (powdered) sugar

### FOR THE COATING:
50g (¼ cup) granulated sugar
1 tsp ground cinnamon

01 In a small bowl, cream together the butter, light brown sugar and cinnamon to make a paste.

02 Cut the crusts off the slices of bread, then roll the bread out flat with a rolling pin. Spread the cinnamon butter all the way to the edges. Roll the bread up nice and tightly from the short edge – the butter should hold the rolls together.

03 In a medium mixing bowl, beat together the eggs, milk and vanilla extract until combined, then dip the rolls in the mix so they're fully covered; you don't need to soak them.

04 Melt a knob of butter in a large frying pan and toast them over a low heat until golden brown on each side.

05 While they're cooking, make the cream cheese frosting. Mix together the butter, cream cheese and icing (powdered) sugar in a small bowl until smooth and combined. You can do this with a spoon or an electric hand mixer is quicker.

06 For the coating, mix together sugar and cinnamon in a bowl, then coat the rolls in the mix while they're still hot. Put the frosting in a pot to dip, or place the rolls on a plate, then transfer the frosting to a piping bag and drizzle it over the top. Serve straight away and enjoy!

Store any leftover cinnamon sugar in a sealed container at room temperature, and leftover cinnamon butter or frosting in a sealed container in the refrigerator.

# JAM DOUGHNUT FRENCH TOAST ROLLS

## Makes 8

French toast rolls crossed with a jam doughnut! They're soft and doughy, filled with fruity jam and rolled in sugar, with all the flavours of a jam doughnut in French toast form. Delicious!

### 15 minutes

8 slices of soft bread
8 tsp of your favourite jam
2 large eggs
60ml (4 tbsp) milk
1 tsp vanilla extract
Knob of butter, for frying
50g (¼ cup) granulated sugar

01  Cut the crusts off the slices of bread, then roll the bread out flat with a rolling pin. Spread the jam all the way to the edges. Roll the bread up nice and tightly from the short edge – the jam should hold the rolls together.

02  In a medium mixing bowl, beat together the eggs, milk and vanilla extract until combined, then dip the rolls in the mix so they're fully covered; you don't need to soak them.

03  Melt a knob of butter in a large frying pan and toast the rolls over a low heat until golden brown on each side.

04  Put the sugar into a bowl and coat the rolls while they're still hot. Serve straight away with whatever you wish. Enjoy!

FAN FAVOURITE · FAN FAVOURITE ·

# CINNAMON ROLL PANCAKES

## Makes 6

These pancakes are thick and fluffy with a sweet cinnamon swirl in the middle. The sugar caramelises when cooking, making these pancakes taste even better! Drizzled with sweet cream cheese frosting, they taste just like cinnamon rolls in pancake form.

## 30 minutes

### FOR THE PANCAKE BATTER:

30g (2 tbsp) unsalted butter, melted and cooled slightly

1 large egg, lightly beaten, at room temperature

110ml (scant ½ cup) whole or semi-skimmed milk, at room temperature

120g (scant ½ cup) plain (all-purpose) flour

25g (2 tbsp) caster (superfine) sugar

2 tsp baking powder

¼ tsp salt

Knob of butter or cooking oil spray, for frying

### FOR THE CINNAMON SWIRL:

30g (2 tbsp) unsalted butter, melted and cooled

40g (3 tbsp) light brown sugar

2 tsp ground cinnamon

### FOR THE CREAM CHEESE FROSTING:

30g (2 tbsp) full-fat cream cheese, at room temperature

30g (2 tbsp) unsalted butter, softened

40g (5 tbsp) icing (powdered) sugar

### FOR THE PANCAKE BATTER:

01 In a medium mixing bowl, mix the melted butter, egg and milk with a balloon whisk until combined.

02 In a separate large mixing bowl, beat together the flour, sugar, baking powder and salt, then make a well in the middle.

03 Gradually pour the wet mix into the dry, mixing gently by hand as you pour until everything comes together and the batter is smooth and lump-free. Leave the batter to rest for 10 minutes.

### FOR THE CINNAMON SWIRL:

04 Mix together the melted butter, light brown sugar and cinnamon in a small mixing bowl until combined, then mix in 1 tablespoon of the pancake batter. Pour into a piping bag.

### TO COOK:

05 Lightly coat a large nonstick frying pan with butter, or spray with oil. Dollop approximately one quarter cup of the pancake batter into the pan. Snip the end off the piping bag to create a small 0.5cm (¼in) opening and swirl the cinnamon mix onto the pancake. Make sure you don't pipe it too close to the edge as it can overspill as it melts.

06 Once bubbles start to form in the pancake batter, flip it over with a large spatula (it should be golden brown) and cook on the other side. The pancakes usually take 1–2 minutes to cook on each side. Carefully lift out of the pan and keep warm while you repeat to make 6 pancakes.

### FOR THE CREAM CHEESE FROSTING:

07 While the pancakes are cooking, or just afterwards, in a small mixing bowl, mix together the cream cheese, softened butter and icing sugar until smooth and creamy, then transfer to a piping bag and pipe over the pancakes, or spread over however you wish. Serve straight away. Enjoy!

FAN FAVOURITE · FAN FAVOURITE ·

# STUFFED MINI PANCAKES

## Makes 12

Soft, thick and fluffy mini pancakes stuffed with chocolate hazelnut spread. These little pancakes make the perfect bite for a fun breakfast or dessert. They're super versatile to stuff with whatever you wish and they're ideal for Pancake Day!

### 30 minutes

105g (generous ¾ cup) self-raising flour

½ tbsp caster (superfine) sugar

¾ tsp baking powder

2 small eggs, at room temperature

12g (¾ tbsp) unsalted butter, melted

85ml (⅓ cup) whole or semi-skimmed milk, at room temperature

Knob of butter or cooking oil spray, for frying

½ tsp chocolate hazelnut spread (I use Nutella) per pancake

### TO SERVE (OPTIONAL)

Chocolate hazelnut spread, melted

Icing (powdered) sugar, for dusting

01  In a large mixing bowl, using a balloon whisk, mix together the flour, sugar and baking powder until combined, then make a well in the middle with the back of a spoon.

02  Add the eggs, melted butter and milk, and beat until smooth and lump-free, then leave the batter to rest for 10 minutes.

03  Lightly coat a large nonstick frying pan with butter, or spray with oil. Dollop 1 tablespoon of the batter onto the pan, then dollop ½ teaspoon of chocolate hazelnut spread into the middle of the pancake and cover with 1 teaspoon of batter.

04  Flip once bubbles form and cook on the other side. They should take roughly 1 minute to cook and should be golden brown. Carefully slide out of the pan and keep warm while you repeat to make about 12 mini pancakes.

05  Drizzle with melted chocolate hazelnut spread and dust with icing (powdered) sugar, or serve however you wish. Enjoy!

# IN THE
# AIR FRYER

# SUPER EXCITING!

Okay, okay... I know I said this was a 'no-bake' book so you might be thinking having an air fryer chapter is cheating a little... but I thought I'd throw some air fryer recipes in there anyway. It's technically not using an oven, so I decided it was acceptable.

This chapter is super exciting for me (and hopefully for you too) because it has some savoury recipes! You'll find Cheese Scones (page 220), a Chicken Tenders Wraps (page 204), Garlic Bread (page 215) and even a Personal Pizza (page 208) in here, alongside some fan favourites including Strawberries and Cream Puffs (page 197), mini Chocolate Cake Pots (page 190) and French Toast Sticks (page 198).

All of these recipes are quick and easy to make and great for cooking in the air fryer to save time and energy, but also for that perfect crispy texture.

Now, I'm going to whisper this part... If you don't have an air fryer, each of the recipes has oven directions too, but don't tell anyone, as this is a no-baking book. I just didn't want to leave out anyone who doesn't own an air fryer.

## HERE ARE SOME TOP TIPS FOR COOKING IN THE AIR FRYER:

♥ **All air fryers are different:** Let's be real, they're just mini fan ovens, so anything you can cook in the oven you can cook in the air fryer and vice versa. That means you should treat it like an oven and **treat all cooking times as a guide.** Especially when it comes to things like chicken, make sure it's cooked through properly.

♥ **Size:** The bigger the better in my opinion, but I understand not everyone wants a large air fryer. How much you can cook at once will depend on the size of your air fryer. My quantities and times are based on an 11-litre air fryer. All the recipes will work with a smaller air fryer, but you may need to cook them in more batches.

♥ **Materials:** Be sure to always use ovenproof materials. The material, shape and size of what you're cooking in (such as a ramekin) will make a difference to how your recipe cooks.

Quick and easy!

# CHOCOLATE CAKE POTS

### Makes 2
~~

These little chocolate cakes are so soft and moist. The glaze is super simple, but just so good, and its sweetness complements the cake perfectly. They're easy to make and cook in just 15 minutes in the air fryer.

**25 minutes**
*+ 30 minutes cooling*

### FOR THE CAKE:
50g (5½ tbsp) plain (all-purpose) flour
35g (2 tbsp) granulated sugar
20g (8 tsp) cocoa powder
½ tsp baking powder
30g (2 tbsp) unsalted butter, melted, or 2 tbsp vegetable oil
125ml (½ cup) warm water

### FOR THE GLAZE:
30g (4 tbsp) icing (powdered) sugar
10g (4 tsp) cocoa powder
About 1 tbsp milk
Chocolate sprinkles, to decorate (optional)

### FOR THE CAKE:
01   Preheat your air fryer to 140°C (275°F).

02   In a small mixing bowl, beat together the flour, sugar, cocoa powder and baking powder until combined.

03   Pour in the melted butter or vegetable oil and warm water and mix until smooth.

04   Divide the mix into 2 ramekins, then bake in the air fryer for 15 minutes, or until a toothpick inserted into the centre comes out with a few moist crumbs on. Leave to cool for at least 30 minutes, then remove from the ramekins if you wish.

### FOR THE GLAZE:
05   Put the icing (powdered) sugar, cocoa powder and milk into a small mixing bowl and mix until smooth. The glaze should be thick, but still pourable. Add more milk if it's too thick or more icing sugar if it's too runny.

06   Pour the glaze over the cakes, then top with chocolate sprinkles, if you like, and enjoy!

07   Store in an airtight container at room temperature for up to 3 days.

### TO BAKE IN THE OVEN:
Cook at 180°C (160°C fan)/350°F/Gas mark 4 for 15–20 minutes.

FAN FAVOURITE · FAN FAVOURITE ·

# STRAWBERRY CHEESECAKE DANISHES

## Makes 8

These Danishes are one of my favourite recipes. The pastry is crisp and flaky, the filling is sweet and creamy and the strawberries are fresh and juicy. They're fun and easy to make and they taste amazing on a summer day (or any day, to be honest).

## 20 minutes

1 sheet of ready-rolled puff pastry
120g (8½ tbsp) full-fat cream cheese, at room temperature
30g (4 tbsp) icing (powdered) sugar
1 tsp vanilla extract
About 4 large fresh strawberries, thinly sliced
1 small egg + 1 tsp water or milk, for the egg wash
Granulated sugar, for sprinkling

### FOR THE GLAZE:
40g (5 tbsp) icing (powdered) sugar + extra for dusting (optional)
About 1 tbsp milk

01 Remove the puff pastry from the refrigerator and leave at room temperature for 10–20 minutes so it's easier to unravel.

02 Preheat the air fryer to 160°C (325°F) and place a piece of nonstick baking paper over your air fryer rack or in the basket.

03 In a medium mixing bowl, beat the cream cheese, icing (powdered) sugar and vanilla extract until smooth and creamy.

04 Unravel the puff pastry and cut it into 8 rectangles (cut in half vertically, in half horizontally, then in half horizontally again, and again to make 8). Score a 1cm (½in) border inside each rectangle, then spread one-eighth of the cream cheese mixture inside the border and place 3 slices of strawberry on each.

05 Beat the egg with the water or milk to make the egg wash, then brush it over the pastry border and sprinkle with the sugar.

06 Transfer the individual pastries onto your prepared baking paper making sure they're at least 2.5cm (1in) apart. It's likely you will only be able to fit 2 on your air fryer rack at a time, so store the rest in the refrigerator until you can bake them, as they will become harder to handle when warm.

07 Air fry for 8–10 minutes until the edges are puffed and golden brown. Leave to cool slightly, then make the glaze. Mix together the icing (powdered) sugar and milk until thick and smooth. Add more icing sugar to make it thicker, or more milk to make it thinner.

08 Transfer the glaze to a piping bag or just use a spoon to drizzle it over the cooled pastries and dust with icing sugar if you wish.

09 Best served fresh on the same day. Enjoy!

If you want to make just 2 Danishes, divide all the ingredients by 4.

### TO BAKE IN THE OVEN:
Cook at 200°C (180°C fan)/400°F/Gas mark 6 for 10–12 minutes.

# BROWNIE CUPS

## Makes 2

These brownie cups are so gooey and chocolatey! They're warm and best eaten with a spoon. They're easy to make with just a few ingredients and they're ready in less than half an hour.

### 25 minutes
### + 10 minutes cooling

80g (2.75oz) dark chocolate
55g (3½ tbsp) salted butter
1 medium egg, room temperature
55g (¼ cup) caster (superfine) sugar
30g (3½ tbsp) plain (all-purpose) flour
½ tsp salt
25g (1½ tbsp) milk or dark chocolate chips + more for the top (optional)

01  In a small microwave-safe mixing bowl, melt the chocolate and butter in 30-second bursts, stirring in between until smooth, then leave to cool for 10 minutes.

02  Preheat your air fryer to 160°C (325°F).

03  Once cool, add the egg and sugar and beat until combined; it should be thick and gloopy.

04  Add the flour and salt and fold it in with a spoon until just combined, then fold in the chocolate chips.

05  Divide the batter into 2 ramekins and smooth it out, then sprinkle with more chocolate chips, if you wish.

06  Place in the centre of your air fryer and bake for 15–18 minutes (cooking times will vary between air fryers).

07  Leave to stand for 2 minutes, then grab a spoon and dig in.

08  Best served straight away, but you can reheat them in the air fryer for 2–3 minutes up to 1 day after baking.

### TO BAKE IN THE OVEN:
Cook at 200°C (180°C fan)/400°F/Gas mark 6 for 20–25 minutes.

# STRAWBERRIES and CREAM PUFFS

FAN FAVOURITE · FAN FAVOURITE

## Makes 10

These puffs taste so fresh and creamy. The puff pastry is light and crisp, filled with strawberry jam, sweet whipped cream and strawberries. Perfect for any garden party or summer barbecue, they're always a favourite.

**20 minutes**
+ cooling

1 sheet of ready-rolled puff pastry
1 small egg + 1 tsp water or milk, for the egg wash
250ml (1 cup) cold double (or heavy) cream
30g (4 tbsp) icing (powdered) sugar + extra for dusting
150g (10 tbsp) strawberry jam
About 5 large fresh strawberries, thinly sliced

If you want to make just 2 puffs, divide all the ingredients by 5.

01 Remove the puff pastry from the refrigerator and leave at room temperature for 10–20 minutes so it's easier to unravel.

02 Preheat the air fryer to 160°C (325°F) and place a piece of nonstick baking paper over your air fryer rack or in the basket.

03 Unravel the puff pastry sheet and cut it into 10 rectangles (cut in half vertically, then horizontally into 5 equal sections).

04 Transfer the individual pastries onto your prepared baking paper making sure they're at least 2.5cm (1in) apart. It's likely you will only be able to fit 2–3 on your air fryer rack at a time, so store the rest in the refrigerator until you're ready to bake them, as they will become harder to handle when warm.

05 Beat the egg with the water or milk until combined to make the egg wash, then brush it over the pastries.

06 Air fry for 7–9 minutes, or until they're puffed and golden, then leave to cool while you bake the rest of the pastries. Once they're all cooled, cut in half carefully using a serrated knife.

07 In a large mixing bowl, whip the cream and icing (powdered) sugar to stiff peaks, then transfer to a piping bag with your favourite large nozzle.

08 Pipe or spread the strawberry jam over the base of the pastries, then pipe the whipped cream over the top. Place the sliced strawberries on the cream, then the pastry lids carefully on top.

09 Dust with icing sugar and serve straight away.

10 Best served fresh on the same day. Enjoy!

### TO BAKE IN THE OVEN:
Cook at 200°C (180°C fan)/400°F/Gas mark 6 for 8–10 minutes.

FAN FAVOURITE · FAN FAVOURITE ·

# FRENCH TOAST STICKS

## Serves 1

If you don't fancy making your French toast in the pan, let the air fryer work its magic.
They're crispy on the outside and doughy in the middle. They're coated in cinnamon sugar
and perfect for dipping in your favourite sauce or spread.

### 15 minutes

2 thick slices of bread (I used brioche)
1 large egg
80ml (⅓ cup) milk
1 tsp vanilla extract
Cooking oil spray
35g (2 tbsp) granulated sugar
½ tsp ground cinnamon

01 Preheat the air fryer to 180°C (350°F) and place a piece of nonstick baking paper over your air fryer rack or in the basket.

02 Cut the bread into 2.5cm (1in) slices, then into 3 batons; you should have 6 batons in total.

03 In a medium mixing bowl, beat together the egg, milk and vanilla extract until combined.

04 Dunk the batons in the mix; you don't need to soak them.

05 Place the batons onto the baking paper, then lightly spray with cooking oil.

06 Air fry them for 8–10 minutes, carefully turning them over halfway through cooking.

07 While they're cooking, mix together the sugar and cinnamon in a bowl.

08 Coat the hot batons in the cinnamon sugar on each side and serve with whatever you wish. I like to dunk or drizzle mine in maple syrup. Enjoy!

### TO BAKE IN THE OVEN:
Cook at 220°C (200°C fan)/425°F/Gas mark 7 for 12–15 minutes.

# COOKIE CUPS

## Makes 2

Sometimes you just want a soft and warm chocolate chip cookie all to yourself to eat with a spoon. These cookie cups have a crisp top and a gooey middle. They're quick and easy to make in the air fryer and they're ready in 20 minutes.

## 20 minutes

50g (3½ tbsp) unsalted butter, softened
40g (3 tbsp) light brown sugar
20g (1 tbsp + 1 tsp) granulated sugar
1 egg yolk
½ tsp vanilla extract
70g (½ cup) plain (all-purpose) flour
¼ tsp bicarbonate of soda (baking soda)
¼ tsp salt
60g (4½ tbsp) chocolate chips + extra for the top

01  Preheat your air fryer to 160°C (325°F).

02  In a small mixing bowl, beat the butter and both sugars with a spoon to form a paste.

03  Add the egg yolk and vanilla extract and mix until combined, then fold in the flour, bicarbonate of soda (baking soda) and salt until just combined. Don't overmix.

04  Fold in the chocolate chips, then divide the dough between 2 ramekins and sprinkle more chocolate chips on top.

05  Place in the centre of your air fryer and bake for 10–15 minutes (cooking times will vary between air fryers).

06  Leave to stand for 2 minutes, then grab a spoon and dig in.

07  Best served straight away, but you can reheat them in the air fryer for 2–3 minutes up to 1 day after baking.

### TO BAKE IN THE OVEN:
Cook at 200°C (180°C fan)/400°F/Gas mark 6 for 15–20 minutes.

# THE EASIEST BAGELS

## Makes 2
~~

Make your own bagels at home with this super-easy 2-ingredient dough. They're soft, doughy and chewy and you can season them however you wish. I chose to make an 'everything bagel seasoning' which goes with almost anything (unless you want to make them sweet, then maybe skip the seasoning).

## 25 minutes

155g (⅔ cup) Greek yogurt
(I use Fage 0% fat)
130g (1 cup) self-raising flour
+ extra for dusting
1 small egg + 1 tsp water or milk,
for the egg wash

### FOR THE 'EVERYTHING BAGEL' SEASONING:
1½ tbsp white sesame seeds,
toasted
1½ tbsp black sesame seeds,
toasted
1 tbsp poppy seeds
1 tbsp onion granules or powder
1 tbsp garlic granules or powder
1 tbsp coarse sea salt

01 Preheat the air fryer to 180°C (350°F).

02 In a medium mixing bowl, mix together the yogurt and flour with a spoon until it comes together, then knead it with your hands until it forms a smooth dough. If it's too sticky, add a little more flour and flour your hands.

03 Flour your surface and cut the dough in half, then press it into 2 bagel shapes. I find it easiest to roll it into a flat doughnut shape, then push a hole through the middle. You want the bagels to be slightly thin and flat before baking, as they will rise and the holes will become smaller.

04 Place the bagels on your air fryer rack or in the basket, then beat the egg with the water or milk until combined to make the egg wash and brush it over the bagels.

05 Make the 'everything bagel' seasoning by adding all the ingredients to a small bowl and mixing them together.

06 Sprinkle as much of the seasoning as you like over the bagels, then store the remaining seasoning in an airtight container to use the next time.

07 Air fry for 13–15 minutes until the tops are golden brown and the bagels have risen.

08 Leave to cool for about 30 minutes, as they will be very hot, then slice and serve however you wish.

09 Best served on the day of baking, but can also be eaten up to the next day if stored in an airtight container. Enjoy!

### TO BAKE IN THE OVEN:
Cook at 220°C (200°C fan)/425°F/Gas mark 7 for 18–20 minutes.

# CHICKEN TENDERS WRAPS

### Makes 2

This recipe is a bit of a two-in-one, as you can serve the chicken tenders with whatever you wish. They're crispy and crunchy on the outside and juicy on the inside. The wrap is packed with fresh lettuce, tomatoes, cheese and the most amazing tangy, creamy sauce! It is such a great lunch or dinner, plus it's really quick and easy to make.

## 20 minutes

30g (3½ tbsp) plain (all-purpose)
 flour
1 tsp salt
¼ tsp pepper
2 tsp paprika
1 large egg
80g (2.75oz) flavoured tortilla
 chips (any flavour you like;
 I use Doritos)
6 chicken breast mini fillets
 (about 300g/10.5oz)

### FOR THE SAUCE:
30ml (2 tbsp) mayonnaise
2 tsp ketchup
2 tsp yellow mustard
Pinch of salt
½ tsp paprika
¼ tsp cayenne pepper

### FOR THE WRAPS:
2 large tortillas
1 medium tomato, chopped into
 small pieces
Handful of iceberg lettuce,
 shredded
30g (1.5oz) cheese of your choice,
 grated (I use Cheddar)

### FOR THE CHICKEN TENDERS:

01 Preheat the air fryer to 180°C (350°F).

02 In a medium bowl, mix together the flour, salt, pepper and paprika until combined.

03 In another bowl, beat the egg well.

04 Put the tortilla chips into a food processor and process until finely crushed. Alternatively, put them into a plastic bag and crush with a rolling pin. Pour into a bowl.

05 Coat the chicken fillets, one by one, in the flour mix, then in the egg, letting any excess drip off, then in the crushed tortilla chips, making sure you pat these on really firmly on both sides of the chicken.

06 Transfer the coated chicken fillets to the air fryer rack or basket, making sure they're not touching each other, and air fry for 10–12 minutes, or until the chicken is cooked through to at least 75°C (203°F), when tested with a meat thermometer.

### FOR THE SAUCE:

07 In a small bowl, mix together the mayonnaise, ketchup, mustard, salt, paprika and cayenne pepper with a spoon until combined. It should be creamy and pale orange in colour.

### FOR THE WRAPS:

08 Chop the cooked chicken into 1cm (½in) cubes.

09 Place the tortillas on a clean surface and place half the chicken in the middle of each. Drizzle the sauce on top, followed by the tomato, lettuce and cheese.

10 Fold your tortillas in from the bottom and the top, then wrap the sides in really tightly; you may need to squeeze the filling together a fair bit to get a nice tight wrap.

11   Heat a frying pan over a medium heat, then place the wraps, overlap side down, in the pan and toast them and hold them together. Once browned, turn them over and toast on the other side until crisp.

12   Use a serrated knife to cut them in half. Serve straight away!

### TO BAKE IN THE OVEN:
Cook at 220˚C (200˚C fan)/425˚F/Gas mark 7 for 12–15 minutes.

# PIZZA TURNOVERS

### Makes 6

These pizza turnovers are so delicious and make a great snack or party food. They're super versatile and you can fill them with whatever pizza toppings you like. I chose cheese, tomato and pepperoni, but why not try a barbecue chicken version as well?

## 20 minutes

1 sheet of ready-rolled puff pastry
90ml (6 tbsp) pizza sauce or passata
160g (12 tbsp) grated mozzarella cheese
6 pieces of pepperoni, chopped
1 tsp dried oregano or Italian herbs
1 small egg + 1 tsp water or milk, for the egg wash

01 Remove the puff pastry from the refrigerator and leave at room temperature for 10–20 minutes so it's easier to unravel.

02 Preheat the air fryer to 160°C (325°F) and place a piece of nonstick baking paper over the air fryer rack or in the basket.

03 Unravel the puff pastry sheet and cut it into 6 squares (cut in half vertically, then horizontally into 3 equal sections).

04 Score each square diagonally, then spread pizza sauce or passata over one half of each, then top with 2 tablespoons of grated cheese, followed by some chopped pepperoni and a sprinkle of oregano or Italian herbs. Be sure to keep all the ingredients in the middle of the pastry half to ensure the edges seal properly and the filling doesn't ooze out.

05 Fold the other half of the pastry over the top, stretching it over the filling, then press the edges together and seal them with the back of a fork. Prick the top of the pastry to allow the air to escape.

06 Transfer the pastries to the air fryer, making sure they're at least 2cm (¾in) apart, then beat the egg with the water or milk until combined to make the egg wash and brush it evenly over the top of the pastries. It's likely you will only fit 2 pastries in your air fryer at a time, so chill the rest in the refrigerator until you are ready to cook them.

07 Air fry the pastries for 10–12 minutes until they're puffed and golden brown.

08 Best served warm, straight away. Enjoy!

### TO BAKE IN THE OVEN:
Cook at 200°C (180°C fan)/400°F/Gas mark 6 for 12–15 minutes.

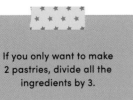

If you only want to make 2 pastries, divide all the ingredients by 3.

# PERSONAL PIZZA

### Makes 1

It's hard to beat homemade pizza. The dough is super easy with just 2 ingredients and it makes the perfect pizza base. Go crazy with your pizza toppings or keep it simple, it's totally up to you. Play around with the dough to create the perfect thickness for you (just make sure it fits inside your air fryer!).

## 25 minutes

75g (5 tbsp) Greek yogurt
(I use Fage 0% fat)
65g (½ cup) self-raising flour
+ extra for dusting
½ tbsp olive oil
60ml (4 tbsp) pizza sauce or
passata
Mozzarella cheese
Dried Italian herbs or oregano
(optional)

01   Preheat the air fryer to 180°C (350°F).

02   In a medium mixing bowl, mix together the Greek yogurt and flour with a spoon until it comes together, then knead it with your hands until it forms a smooth dough. If it's too sticky, add a little more flour and flour your hands.

03   Flour your surface and a rolling pin and roll out the dough to about 0.5cm (¼in) thick and shape it into a circle (make sure it's not too big for your air fryer).

04   Brush the dough with oil on both sides, then place on your air fryer rack or in the basket and air fry for 5 minutes.

05   Remove from the air fryer and spread on the pizza sauce, followed by the cheese, leaving a 1cm (½in) border around the edge.

06   Air fry again for about 10 minutes, or until the cheese has melted and the dough is cooked through.

07   Transfer the pizza onto a serving plate and sprinkle over Italian herbs or oregano, if you wish.

08   Serve warm, straight away. Enjoy!

### TO BAKE IN THE OVEN:
Cook at 220°C (200°C fan)/425°F/Gas mark 7 for 5 minutes before adding your toppings, then a further 12–15 minutes once you've added your toppings.

FAN FAVOURITE · FAN FAVOURITE ·

# POPCORN CHICKEN

## Makes about 30

These popcorn chicken bites are so tasty! They're packed with flavour and the panko breadcrumbs give them that perfect crispy coating. They're super quick in the air fryer and they're great as a snack, party food or as part of a meal.

### 20 minutes

6 chicken breast mini fillets (about 300g/10.5oz), cut into 2.5cm (1in) cubes
½ tsp salt
½ tsp pepper
½ tsp garlic powder
1 tsp paprika
½ tsp onion salt
30g (3½ tbsp) plain (all-purpose) flour
60g (⅔ cup) panko breadcrumbs
1 large egg
Cooking oil spray

01   Preheat the air fryer to 200°C (400°F).

02   Add the chicken cubes to a medium mixing bowl. Then add the salt, pepper, garlic powder, paprika and onion salt and coat the chicken well using your hands (be sure to wash your hands after touching the chicken).

03   Put the flour and panko breadcrumbs into separate bowls, then crack the egg into another bowl and beat it lightly.

04   Coat the chicken pieces in the flour, then in the egg, letting any excess drip off, then in the panko breadcrumbs, pressing them in well.

05   Place the chicken on your air fryer rack or in the basket and spray lightly with cooking oil. Air fry for 6–8 minutes, or until they're cooked through (at least 75°C/203°F when tested with a meat thermometer). You may need to cook them in 2 batches depending on the size of your air fryer.

06   Serve straight away with your favourite sauce and sides and enjoy!

**TO BAKE IN THE OVEN:**
Cook at 220°C (200°C fan)/425°F/Gas mark 7 for 8–10 minutes.

In the Air Fryer

# CHEESY QUESADILLA

## Makes 1

Fun fact, I was given the name 'quesadilla girl' at a café because I ordered them so often! I think it's fair to say I'm a big fan of quesadillas. They're so versatile and they're great to eat at any time of the day (even breakfast). I kept this one simple with cheese and peppers, but feel free to add your favourite fillings and don't forget the dips!

### 10 minutes

2 large tortillas
Grated cheese of your choice
¼ green (bell) pepper and ¼ red (bell) pepper, deseeded and sliced thinly into small chunks
Cooking oil spray

01  Preheat the air fryer to 180°C (350°F).

02  Place 1 tortilla on the air fryer rack or in the basket.

03  Sprinkle the cheese and chopped peppers evenly over the tortilla. Place the other tortilla on top and spray it lightly with cooking oil to make it crispier. You can, if you wish, push a couple of toothpicks into the tortillas to hold them together so they are less likely to blow around in the air fryer.

04  Air fry for 5–7 minutes, flipping the quesadilla over halfway through the cooking.

05  Cut it into triangles and serve warm, straight away with your favourite dips such as guacamole, salsa and sour cream.

#### TO BAKE IN THE OVEN:
Cook at 220°C (200°C fan)/425°F/Gas mark 7 for 7–9 minutes.

If you don't like crunchy peppers, cook them beforehand. You could also add cooked onion, chicken or anything of your choosing.

In the Air Fryer

# GARLIC BREAD

## Makes 4 pieces

Garlic bread is one of my favourite side dishes. It's soft, doughy, buttery and, of course, garlicky. This garlic bread is so easy to make with just a few simple ingredients and it takes only 10 minutes to prep and cook.

## 10 minutes

1 small white baguette or baton
50g (3½ tbsp) salted butter, softened
1 garlic clove, finely minced
1 tsp dried Italian herbs or oregano

01  Preheat the air fryer to 180°C (350°F).

02  Slice the baguette or baton in half horizontally, then lengthways through the middle, to make 4 pieces.

03  Put the butter, garlic and herbs into a small bowl and mash it altogether until fully combined.

04  Spread the garlic butter evenly over the bread slices, then place them on your air fryer rack or in the basket.

05  Air fry for about 5 minutes, or until the edges are light brown and crisp.

06  Serve warm, straight away. Enjoy!

### TO BAKE IN THE OVEN:
Cook at 220°C (200°C fan)/425°F/Gas mark 7 for 5–6 minutes.

215

In the Air Fryer

Sprinkle some mozzarella cheese over your garlic bread before cooking to make cheesy garlic bread.

# MOZZARELLA STICKS

## Serves 2-4
~~

Warm, gooey, and cheesy, in a crispy coating, served with your favourite dip.
These mozzarella sticks taste so delicious and they crisp up perfectly in the air fryer.

**15 minutes**
*+ 1 hour freezing*

200g (7oz) block mozzarella
  cheese
30g (3½ tbsp) plain (all-purpose)
  flour
1 large egg
80g (scant 1 cup) panko
  breadcrumbs
1 tsp paprika
½ tsp garlic granules or powder
½ tsp onion granules or powder

01  Cut the block of cheese into sticks, then place on a freezer-proof plate lined with nonstick baking paper and freeze for 30 minutes.

02  Place the flour into a bowl, then beat the egg in another bowl, and mix the panko breadcrumbs with the paprika, garlic and onion granules or powder in a third bowl.

03  Coat the frozen mozzarella sticks in the flour, then in the egg, letting any excess drip off, then in the panko breadcrumb mix, pressing them in really well.

04  Return them to the plate and freeze for another 30 minutes.

05  Preheat your air fryer to 200°C (400°F), then coat the mozzarella sticks in the egg, again letting any excess drip off, then in the panko breadcrumb mix one more time.

06  Place the mozzarella sticks on your air fryer rack or in the basket, making sure they're not touching, and air fry for 7–8 minutes until crisp and golden.

07  Serve warm, straight away with your favourite dipping sauce. Enjoy!

### TO BAKE IN THE OVEN:
Cook at 240°C (220°C fan)/475°F/Gas mark 9 for 10–12 minutes.

# HAM and CHEESE PUFFS

## Makes 6

I just love a savoury pastry, there's something about that flaky pastry parcel filled with warm, gooey cheese. Yum! These ham and cheese puffs are so quick and easy to make with just a few ingredients and they're guaranteed to please.

## 20 minutes

1 sheet of ready-rolled puff pastry
160g (12 tbsp) grated Cheddar cheese
100g (3.5oz) cooked ham, chopped into small pieces
1 small egg + 1 tsp water or milk, for the egg wash

In the Air Fryer

01  Remove the puff pastry from the refrigerator and leave at room temperature for 10–20 minutes so it's easier to unravel.

02  Preheat the air fryer to 160°C (325°F) and place a piece of nonstick baking paper over the air fryer rack or in the basket.

03  Unravel the puff pastry sheet and cut it into 6 squares (cut in half vertically, then horizontally into 3 equal sections).

04  Score each square across the middle, then sprinkle 2 tablespoons of cheese over one half of each and top with the chopped ham. Be sure to keep all the ingredients in the middle of the pastry half to ensure the edges seal properly and the filling doesn't ooze out.

05  Fold the other half of the pastry over the top, stretching it over the filling, then press the edges together and seal them with the back of a fork. Prick the top of the pastry a few times to allow the air to escape.

06  Transfer the pastries to the air fryer, making sure they're at least 2cm (¾in) apart, then beat the egg with the water or milk until combined to make the egg wash and brush it evenly over the top of the pastries. It's likely you will only fit 2 pastries in your air fryer at a time, so chill the rest in the refrigerator until ready to cook them.

07  Air fry the pastries for 10–12 minutes until they're puffed and golden brown.

08  Best served warm, straight away. Enjoy!

### TO BAKE IN THE OVEN:
Cook at 200°C (180°C fan)/350°F/Gas mark 6 for 12–15 minutes.

If you only want to make 2 pastries, divide all the ingredients by 3.

# CHEESE SCONES

## Makes 5

I absolutely love cheese scones (to be honest, I love all scones), and these cheese ones taste so good and they're so quick and easy to make. I used to make these a lot with my great auntie and we always ate them smothered in butter. Yum!

## 20 minutes

115g (scant ½ cup) self-raising flour + extra for dusting
30g (2 tbsp) cold salted butter
½ tsp salt
15g (1 scant tbsp) Cheddar cheese, grated
75ml (¼ cup) milk + 1 tbsp for brushing

01  Preheat the air fryer to 180°C (350°F).

02  In a large mixing bowl, mix together the flour, butter and salt with your fingertips until it forms a crumbly breadcrumb texture, then stir in the cheese and the milk with a spoon to form a soft dough.

03  Flour your surface, then gently knead the dough. Pat the dough down so it's about 2cm (¾in) thick, then use a 5cm (2in) crinkle cookie cutter to cut out 5 circles. You may need to re-roll the dough to make 5.

04  Place the scones on your air fryer rack or in the basket. You may need to cook them in 2 batches, depending on the size of your air fryer.

05  Brush the top of the scones with milk, then bake them for 10–12 minutes, or until they're risen and golden brown on top, then leave to cool slightly.

06  Best served fresh with butter. Enjoy!

07  Store in an airtight container for up to 3 days. You can also wrap them in cling film (plastic wrap) and freeze for up to 3 months.

### TO BAKE IN THE OVEN:
Cook at 220°C (200°C fan)/425°F/Gas mark 7 for 12–15 minutes.

Add ½–1 teaspoon of onion powder to make cheese and onion scones.

# SEASONAL

# ALL YEAR ROUND!

It's that time of the year (or one of them anyway)... It's time to do some seasonal 'baking'.

I love how creative you can be around Easter, Halloween and Christmas, and we can't forget about birthdays, which happen all year round, any excuse if you ask me!

This chapter is packed full of fun, themed desserts that will get you excited for that special occasion. Of course, I had to include lots of themed cheesecakes in this chapter, such as a Spiderweb Cheesecake (page 238) for Halloween and the Birthday Cake Cheesecake on page 226 (because not everyone wants cake on their birthday).

Have fun with this chapter and get creative with your decorations. Feel free to use it as inspiration to make your own creations or even mix and match the flavours that you like.

## HERE ARE SOME TOP TIPS FOR THIS CHAPTER:

♥ **Play around with the flavours:** If there's an idea you like the look of, but a flavour you don't like, change it up for something that works for you and use recipes from the other chapters to decorate.

♥ **Make ahead:** Most of these recipes will keep for at least 3 days in the fridge, so feel free to make them ahead, so you can relax on the day.

Any excuse!

FAN FAVOURITE · FAN FAVOURITE ·

# BIRTHDAY CAKE CHEESECAKE

## Serves 16

When you don't want cake on your birthday, why not have cheesecake instead? This cheesecake is definitely a crowd-pleaser and will be the centre of attention at any party. It has a buttery biscuit base, a white chocolate-and-sprinkles cheesecake filling and is topped with a creamy white chocolate ganache and more sprinkles. Don't forget the candles!

### 30 minutes
+ 7 hours chilling

### FOR THE BASE:
350g (12.4oz) vanilla sandwich biscuits (I use custard creams or Golden Oreos)
150g (5.25oz) unsalted or salted butter, melted

### FOR THE FILLING:
300ml (1¼ cups) cold double (or heavy) cream
500g (1lb) full-fat cream cheese, at room temperature
120g (1 cup) icing (powdered) sugar
1 tsp vanilla extract
250g (9oz) white chocolate, melted and cooled slightly
3–4 tbsp sprinkles

### FOR THE TOPPING:
200g (7oz) white chocolate, broken into pieces
125ml (½ cup) double (or heavy) cream
Handful of sprinkles

### FOR THE BASE:

01   Line the bottom of a 20cm (8in) round springform cake tin with a circle of nonstick baking paper.

02   Put the biscuits into a food processor and process until finely crushed. Alternatively, put them into a plastic bag and crush with a rolling pin. Tip into a large mixing bowl, then pour in the melted butter and mix with a spoon until fully combined. Press the mixture firmly into the bottom of your prepared tin with the back of a spoon, then pop into the refrigerator while you make the filling.

### FOR THE FILLING:

03   In a large mixing bowl, whip the cream with an electric hand mixer until stiff peaks form. In a separate large bowl, beat together the cream cheese, icing (powdered) sugar, vanilla extract and melted white chocolate with the electric mixer until just combined.

04   Fold in the whipped cream with a rubber spatula until just combined, then fold in the sprinkles. Be careful not to overmix as this can make the cheesecake go runny.

05   Remove the chilled base from the refrigerator, then spoon in the filling, smoothing it out to the edges and pressing it down onto the base to avoid any gaps. Chill in the refrigerator for at least 6 hours, or overnight, if possible, until completely set.

### FOR THE TOPPING:

06   When ready to decorate, put the white chocolate pieces and cream into a microwave-safe bowl and microwave on high for 1 minute 20 seconds (the cream should be warm enough to melt the chocolate without boiling and curdling). Leave to stand for about 2 minutes, then stir until the cream and chocolate start to come together. Continue to stir until smooth and creamy, then leave it to cool until it's lukewarm to touch but still pourable.

07    Remove the cheesecake from the tin and transfer to a wire
      rack, then pour the ganache over the top, spreading it out
      quickly with the back of a metal spoon or a spatula, allowing
      it to drip over the edges slightly. Return it to the refrigerator
      for 1 hour, or until the topping has fully set, then decorate with
      sprinkles around the edge. (Don't forget the candles too!)

08    Serve straight away or store in the refrigerator for up to 3 days.

# VALENTINE'S CHOCOLATE BARK

## Serves 12-16

If you're looking for something easy and fun to make on Valentine's Day, this is for you. Get creative and see what Valentine's Day-themed decorations you can find. I used white chocolate, but feel free to use milk or dark chocolate as the base to make it your own.

### 10 minutes
### + 1-2 hours setting

400g (14oz) white chocolate
Pink or red food colouring
Freeze-dried strawberries
    or raspberries
Pink sprinkles, heart shapes
    if you can find them
Any other Valentine's Day-themed
    chocolate or candies

01  Temper the white chocolate (see page 14).

02  Dab small blobs of the melted white chocolate in the corners of a shallow 23 x 33cm (9 x 13in) tin, then place a sheet of nonstick baking paper on top. The chocolate will set and hold it in place.

03  Transfer a quarter (100g/3.5oz) of the tempered white chocolate to a separate bowl and mix with a small amount of food colouring to turn it pink.

04  Pour the remaining white chocolate onto the tin and smooth it out to the edges; it should be around 1cm (½in) thick.

05  Drizzle the pink white chocolate over the top, then swirl it through with a skewer or knife to make a pretty pattern.

06  Decorate with the freeze-dried strawberries or raspberries, sprinkles and any other chocolates or candies however you wish. Use the photo as a guide.

07  Leave to set at room temperature for 1–2 hours, then cut or break into pieces and enjoy!

08  Store at room temperature for up to 1 week or in the refrigerator for up to 1 month.

Make sure you use the correct food colouring to colour the chocolate (see page 11).

# VALENTINE'S SALTED CARAMEL GANACHE POTS

## Makes 3-4

If chocolate is your love language, I got you... because me too. These chocolate ganache pots are easy to make and soooo chocolatey with a pocket of salted caramel in the middle. The perfect dessert for Valentine's Day.

### 10 minutes
#### + 2 hours chilling

200ml (scant 1 cup) double (or heavy) cream

40g (3 tbsp) caster (superfine) sugar

⅛ tsp salt

1 tsp vanilla extract

95g (3oz) dark chocolate, coarsely chopped

3–4 tbsp thick ready-made salted caramel sauce (I use Sainsbury's Taste the Difference Salted Caramel Sauce)

Flaky sea salt, chocolate curls or gold or bronze sprinkles, to decorate (optional)

01  Put the cream, sugar, salt and vanilla extract into a medium microwave-safe jug. Microwave on high for 1 minute, then stir until the sugar has dissolved.

02  Put the chocolate into a medium mixing bowl, then pour the cream mixture over the top and stir gently until the chocolate melts and it becomes smooth.

03  Pour half the chocolate mixture into 3 or 4 small ramekins or pots, then dollop 1 tablespoon of caramel in the middle of each and pour the remaining chocolate mixture on top.

04  Chill in the refrigerator for at least 2 hours, then decorate with flaky sea salt, chocolate curls or sprinkles, if you like, and serve cold. Enjoy!

05  Store covered in the refrigerator for up to 3 days.

# CHOCOLATE CORNFLAKE NESTS

## Makes 12

These take me back to my childhood, baking with my great auntie around Easter time. I'm sure more of the mixture made it into my mouth than made it into the cupcake cases, but that's all part of the fun. This is always a highly requested recipe around Easter, so now you have the recipe to hand.

**10 minutes**
*+ 1 hour chilling*

200g (7oz) milk chocolate, broken into pieces
75ml (5 tbsp) golden syrup or honey
100g (3.5oz) salted butter
120g (4½ cups) cornflakes
36 mini chocolate eggs

01 Line a 12-hole cupcake tin with cupcake cases.

02 Put the chocolate, golden syrup or honey and butter into a large microwave-safe mixing bowl and melt on medium in 40-second bursts, stirring in between until smooth. You could also use a double boiler (see pages 13–14).

03 Pour the cornflakes into the bowl and stir gently until they're fully coated.

04 Divide the mixture between the 12 cases, pressing the middle down slightly to create a nest shape, then place 3 eggs in the middle of each.

05 Chill in the refrigerator for 1 hour until set and enjoy!

06 Store in the refrigerator for up to 3 days.

233

Seasonal

# CHOCOLATE EGG CHEESECAKE

## Serves 16
~~

The perfect Easter dessert, this Easter egg cheesecake has a buttery biscuit base, a creamy vanilla cheesecake filling, is packed with crushed chocolate eggs and topped with sweet whipped cream and lots and lots of colourful chocolate eggs.

**30 minutes**
**+ 6 hours chilling**

### FOR THE BASE:
350g (12.4oz) digestive biscuits (or graham crackers)
180g (6oz) salted butter, melted

### FOR THE FILLING:
400ml (1⅔ cups) cold double (or heavy) cream
500g (1lb) full-fat cream cheese, at room temperature
120g (1 cup) icing (powdered) sugar
2 tsp vanilla extract
100g (3.5oz) mini eggs, crushed

### FOR THE TOPPING:
150ml (⅔ cup) cold double (or heavy) cream
30g (4 tbsp) icing (powdered) sugar
150g (5.25oz) mini eggs, 16 kept whole, the remaining chopped

### FOR THE BASE:
01 Line the bottom of a 20cm (8in) round springform cake tin with a circle of nonstick baking paper.

02 Put the biscuits into a food processor and process until finely crushed. Alternatively, put them into a plastic bag and crush with a rolling pin. Tip into a large mixing bowl, then pour in the melted butter and mix with a spoon until fully combined. Press the mixture firmly into the bottom of your prepared tin with the back of a spoon, then pop into the refrigerator while you make the filling.

### FOR THE FILLING:
03 In a large mixing bowl, whip the cream with an electric hand mixer until stiff peaks form. In a separate large bowl, beat together the cream cheese, icing (powdered) sugar and vanilla extract with the electric mixer until just combined.

04 Fold in the whipped cream with a rubber spatula until just combined, then fold in the crushed mini eggs. Be careful not to overmix as this can make the cheesecake go runny.

05 Remove the chilled base from the refrigerator, then spoon in the filling, smoothing it out to the edges and pressing it down onto the base to avoid any gaps. Chill in the refrigerator for at least 6 hours, or overnight, if possible, until completely set.

### FOR THE TOPPING:
06 Remove the cheesecake from the tin and transfer onto a serving plate. Whip the cream and icing sugar to stiff peaks using an electric mixer and transfer into a piping bag with your favourite piping nozzle.

07 To decorate, pipe 16 swirls of cream around the edge of the cheesecake and place a whole mini egg on top of each. Place the chopped mini eggs in the middle of the cheesecake (see the photo for inspiration).

08 Store in the refrigerator for up to 3 days.

# SPOOKY MUMMY BARK

## Serves 12-16

This is such a fun one to make around Halloween. It's super quick and easy to produce and it's great on the table at parties or to put into goody bags for everyone to take away. It's packed with cookies and cream biscuits, and don't forget the edible eyes.

### 10 minutes
**+ 1-2 hours setting**

300g (10.5oz) white chocolate
+ 50g (1.75oz) for the drizzle
14 cookies and cream biscuits
(I use Oreos), broken into pieces
About 14 pairs of edible eyes

01 Temper the white chocolate (see page 14).

02 Dab small blobs of the tempered white chocolate in the corners of a shallow 23 x 33cm (9 x 13in) tin, then place a sheet of nonstick baking paper on top. The chocolate will set and hold it in place.

03 Transfer around 50g (1.75oz) of the melted chocolate into a piping bag.

04 Stir the broken biscuits into the bowl of white chocolate until coated, then scoop the mix into the tin and spread it out evenly to the edges.

05 Snip the end off the piping bag to create a 0.5cm (¼in) opening, then pipe chocolate over the top, horizontally and diagonally. Place edible eyes in pairs on the chocolate however you wish. Use the photo as a guide.

06 Let it set at room temperature for around 1–2 hours, then cut or break into pieces and enjoy!

07 Store in an airtight container at room temperature for up to 4 days.

You can store it in the refrigerator if your room is really warm, but be aware this can make the edible eyes run.

# SPIDERWEB CHEESECAKE

## Serves 16

This one doesn't just look amazing, it tastes amazing too! It has a crunchy cookies and cream base, a creamy cookies and cream cheesecake filling, topped with a rich dark chocolate ganache and glazed with a white chocolate spiderweb. It's so much easier to make than you might think and it will look great at any Halloween party.

**25 minutes**
+ 5 hours chilling

### FOR THE BASE:
230g (8.5oz) cookies and cream biscuits (I use Oreos)
60g (4 tbsp) salted butter, melted

### FOR THE FILLING:
500g (1lb) full-fat cream cheese, at room temperature
120g (1 cup) icing (powdered) sugar
10 cookies and cream biscuits, broken into small chunks

### FOR THE DARK CHOCOLATE GANACHE:
150g (5.25oz) dark chocolate, broken into pieces
150ml (⅔ cup) double (or heavy) cream

### FOR THE WHITE CHOCOLATE GANACHE:
40g (1.5oz) white chocolate, broken into pieces
30ml (2 tbsp) double (or heavy) cream

### FOR THE BASE:
01  Line a 20cm (8in) square baking tin with nonstick baking paper.

02  Put the biscuits into a food processor and process until finely crushed. Alternatively, put them into a plastic bag and crush with a rolling pin. Tip into a medium mixing bowl, then pour in the melted butter and mix with a spoon until fully combined.

03  Press the mixture firmly into the bottom of your prepared tin with the back of a spoon, then pop into the refrigerator while you make the filling.

### FOR THE FILLING:
04  In a large mixing bowl, beat together the cream cheese and icing (powdered) sugar with an electric hand mixer until smooth, then fold in the broken biscuits. Remove the chilled base from the refrigerator, then spoon on the filling, smoothing it out to the edges.

05  Chill in the refrigerator for at least 4 hours, or until set.

### FOR THE TOPPING:
06  When the cheesecake has set, put the dark chocolate pieces and cream into a microwave-safe bowl and microwave on high for 1 minute 20 seconds (the cream should be warm enough to melt the chocolate without boiling and curdling). Leave to stand for about 2 minutes, then gently stir until the cream and chocolate start to come together. Continue to stir until smooth and creamy. Repeat this with the white chocolate and cream, but microwave in 20-second bursts on low, as it is such a small amount.

07  Remove the cheesecake from the tin and transfer to a serving plate, then pour the dark chocolate ganache over the top and smooth it out quickly with the back of a metal spoon or a spatula, letting it drip over the edges slightly.

**08** Transfer the white chocolate ganache to a piping bag and snip a small hole at the bottom. Pipe a tight spiral, starting from the upper left quadrant of the cake. Drag a toothpick or skewer outwards through the chocolate, starting from the middle of the spiral. This will create a web look.

**09** Let it set in the refrigerator for at least 1 hour and serve. Enjoy!

**10** Store in the refrigerator for up to 3 days.

# GINGERBREAD TRIFLE

## Serves 12
~~

This trifle is the perfect Christmas dessert if Christmas pudding isn't really your thing, or if you're like me and you like to have multiple desserts to choose from. The trifle is packed with little gingerbread cookies, ginger cake, spiced whipped cream, speculoos spread (cookie butter) and festive sprinkles. It's such a showstopper and it's absolutely delicious!

**20 minutes**
+ 1 hour chilling

400g (14oz) store-bought
   ginger cake
500ml (2¼ cups) cold double
   (or heavy) cream
100g (generous ¾ cup) icing
   (powdered) sugar
½ tsp ground ginger
½ tsp ground cinnamon
250g (9oz) gingerbread men
   + extra to decorate (optional)
300g (1¼ cups) speculoos
   spread/cookie butter, melted
   (I use Biscoff)
Festive sprinkles, to decorate
   (optional)

01   Cut the ginger cake into 2cm (¾in) slices.

02   Put the cream, icing (powdered) sugar, ginger and cinnamon into a large mixing bowl and whip using an electric hand mixer until soft peaks form.

03   Place half the cake into the bottom of a 20cm (8in) round x 20cm (8in) deep glass serving dish, then place a third of the gingerbread men around the edge of the dish.

04   Dollop half the whipped cream evenly on top of the cake, spreading it out to the edges, then drizzle half the melted speculoos spread (cookie butter) over the top.

05   Repeat with the remaining cake, gingerbread men, whipped cream and speculoos spread.

06   Decorate with gingerbread men and festival sprinkles if you wish.

07   Chill in the refrigerator for at least 1 hour and enjoy!

08   Store in the refrigerator, covered, for up to 3 days.

FIVE OR LESS
5
FIVE OR LESS

# FESTIVE TRUFFLE TART

### Serves 16

With all the Christmas truffles and chocolates going around at Christmas time, why not use some to make a dessert? This truffle tart is so easy to make, but it looks so impressive. It has a crunchy cookies and cream crust and a rich chocolatey filling, topped with chocolate truffles and festive sprinkles.

## 15 minutes
### + 4 hours chilling

### FOR THE BASE:
350g (12.4oz) cookies and cream biscuits (I use Oreos)
125g (8½ tbsp) unsalted butter, melted

### FOR THE FILLING:
230g (8.5oz) dark chocolate, broken into pieces
280ml (scant 1¼ cups) double (or heavy) cream

### TO DECORATE:
About 20 chocolate truffles (I use Lindt Lindor truffles)
Festive or gold sprinkles (optional)

Seasonal

### FOR THE BASE:
01  Put the biscuits into a food processor and process until finely crushed. Alternatively, put them into a plastic bag and crush with a rolling pin. Tip into a medium mixing bowl, then pour in the melted butter and mix with a spoon until fully combined.

02  Pour into a deep, loose-bottomed 22cm (8½in) pie tin, pressing down firmly into the base and around the edges with the back of a spoon to create your pie crust.

### FOR THE FILLING:
03  Put the chocolate and cream in a microwave-safe bowl or jug and microwave on medium for 1 minute 20 seconds, then leave to stand for 1 minute. Stir the mixture gently until smooth and combined, then pour it onto the base and smooth it out carefully.

### TO DECORATE:
04  Decorate with chocolate truffles and with sprinkles if you like, then chill in the refrigerator for at least 4 hours. Use a hot knife for a nice clean cut.

05  Store in the refrigerator for up to 3 days.

# CHOCOLATE ORANGE CHEESECAKE POTS

## Makes 2

These chocolate orange cheesecake pots make fab individual desserts. They have a buttery biscuit base and a creamy chocolate orange cheesecake filling, topped with a hard chocolate orange shell that you smash with a spoon to dig into.

## 10 minutes
### + 1 hour chilling

### FOR THE BASE:
3 digestive biscuits (or graham crackers)
20g (1½ tbsp) salted or unsalted butter, melted

### FOR THE FILLING:
115g (4oz) full-fat cream cheese, at room temperature
1 tbsp icing (powdered) sugar
20g (0.75oz) chocolate orange + 40g (1.5oz) for the topping, melted

### FOR THE TOPPING:
2 chocolate orange mini segments
Gold or orange sprinkles, to decorate (optional)

### FOR THE BASE:

01  Put the biscuits into a food processor and process until finely crushed. Alternatively, put them into a plastic bag and crush with a rolling pin. Tip into a small mixing bowl, then pour in the melted butter and mix with a spoon until fully combined.

02  Divide the mix between 2 small pots or ramekins and press down gently with the back of a spoon.

### FOR THE FILLING:

03  In a small mixing bowl, beat together the cream cheese, icing (powdered) sugar, and 20g (0.75oz) of melted chocolate orange with an electric hand mixer until smooth, then scoop the mixture onto the bases and spread it out to the edges.

### FOR THE TOPPING:

04  Pour the remaining melted chocolate orange onto each cheesecake and smooth it out to the edges so the cheesecake is completely covered, then decorate with a mini chocolate orange segment and gold or orange sprinkles if you wish.

05  Chill in the refrigerator for at least 1 hour for best results and enjoy!

06  Store in the refrigerator for up to 3 days.

# SNOWBALL TRUFFLES

## Makes 8
~~

These little truffles are sweet, delicious and coconutty and perfect for Christmas time. They're filled with creamy vanilla biscuits, enrobed in white chocolate and covered in coconut. Yum!

### 20 minutes
+ 1 hour chilling

110g (4oz) vanilla sandwich biscuits (I use custard creams or Golden Oreos)

55g (3½ tbsp) full-fat cream cheese, at room temperature

45g (½ cup) desiccated (shredded, dried) coconut

200g (7oz) white chocolate, broken into pieces

01 Put the biscuits into a food processor and process until finely crushed. Alternatively, put them into a plastic bag and crush with a rolling pin. Tip the crushed biscuits into a medium bowl. Add the cream cheese and 1 tablespoon of the coconut and mix with a spoon until fully combined.

02 Scoop up about 1 tablespoon of the mixture, then roll into a ball with your hands and place on a freezer-proof plate. Repeat with the remaining mixture to make 8 truffles, then transfer to the freezer and chill for 30 minutes.

03 When ready to coat, set a sheet of baking paper over a large plate or tray and melt the chocolate (see page 13).

04 Using 2 forks, coat each ball in the melted chocolate mix, letting any excess drip off, then transfer to the prepared baking paper and chill in the refrigerator for 20 minutes.

05 Remove the truffles from the refrigerator and coat them in a very small amount of the remaining white chocolate; you may need to remelt it if it's too hard.

06 Pour the remaining coconut onto a plate or into a bowl, and roll the truffles in the coconut until they're fully covered; then return to the refrigerator for 10 minutes to set fully before serving.

07 Store in an airtight container in the refrigerator for up to 4 days.

# INDEX

# ACKNOWLEDGEMENTS

Whether you're new here or have made it to book number three without getting bored of me yet, THANK YOU! I appreciate you all so very much, your support is my biggest motivation and, without you, this series of books just wouldn't be possible.

A special thank you to my online community, some of you have been following me since 2016 and your messages remind me how far I've come. You are always there to celebrate the wins and milestones and that means so much to me. Over time the meaning of 'Fitwaffle' has adapted various times and the latest meaning is fitting this book on to your book shelves, hopefully alongside books one and two!

I love seeing you all enjoy these recipes, and as much as my husband pesters me to make swanky-looking cakes, I am thankful for you guys encouraging me to keep it simple so everyone can get involved. Keeping it simple and easy has been the at the root of building this community and I appreciate you for joining in on the fun.

Even though this is my third book, I would not know where to start if it wasn't for my wonderful literary agents Eve White, Ludo Cinelli and Steven Evans. They have carefully guided me through each book with the most incredible patience.

Whilst we are on the topic of patience, not a person in this world has displayed such a high level of patience as my editor Emily Brickell. Thank you for bringing yet another book together, I appreciate my deadline discipline can be a bit shaky, but you make it work every time, thank you so so much!

I have an incredible team that steps in to make sure each book looks worthy of your shelves. Thank you to Faith Mason for making the photos so amazing, as always. Thank you to Katie Marshall and her team for making my recipes look perfect every time, and thank you to Faye Wears for the beautiful props and colours. You're the best team anyone could ask for and I absolutely love working with you all. If you're wondering how these books turn out to be so beautiful each time, it's not my doing. Thank you so much to Studio Nic&Lou for the gorgeous designs and bringing each book together.

Thank you to Holly and Jon for venturing into my home, to capture me in my natural habitat (minus the dirty sweatpants). Having my photo taken doesn't come naturally to me, but Holly and Jon make the process so much easier.

Lastly, thank you to Bernie, my wonderful husband and chief recipe taster. His roles are too long to list, but most importantly he stacks a mean dishwasher.

Ebury Press an imprint of Ebury Publishing,
20 Vauxhall Bridge Road,
London SW1V 2SA

Ebury Press is part of the Penguin Random House group of companies
whose addresses can be found at global.penguinrandomhouse.com

Penguin
Random House
UK

Copyright © Eloise Head 2024
Photography except pages 9, 15 and 255 © Faith Mason 2024
Photography on pages 9, 15 and 255 © Holly Pickering 2024

Eloise Head has asserted her right to be identified as the author of this
Work in accordance with the Copyright, Designs and Patents Act 1988

First published by Ebury Press in 2024

www.penguin.co.uk

A CIP catalogue record for this book is available from the British Library

ISBN 9781529921663

Design by Studio Nic&Lou
Food styling by Katie Marshall
Prop styling by Faye Wears

Colour origination by Altaimage Ltd
Printed and bound in Germany by Aprinta Druck GmbH & Co. KG

Penguin Random House is committed to a sustainable future for our
business, our readers and our planet. This book is made from Forest
Stewardship Council® certified paper.